# DISCOVER YOUR MAGICKAL WITCH'S GARDEN

## GUIDE TO DESIGNING, PLANTING & USING YOUR HERBAL SANCTUARY FOR SPELLWORK & REJUVENATION

DELPHINA D'ANDRES

# CONTENTS

# IN MEMORY OF

*My father, George, my best friend and guardian, whose
Leo sun sign brought brightness to those around him, as
well as to his beautiful, bountiful gardens—Dad's passion
in life after his family.
My father was known for his wisdom and fairness and
always reminded me,
"Someone is always doing something somebody said
couldn't be done."*

# INTRODUCTION

*"Being a Witch gives you the power to heal yourself, change your life, change your world, and conjure your every dream."*

— JULIET DIAZ

Are you someone who has always felt a connection to the mystical and magickal world? Have you ever identified as a witch or have the desire to start your witchy garden? If so, then this book is for you.

I'd like to start by telling you a story. Imagine you're walking through a lush garden filled with vibrant flowers, winding paths, and aromatic herbs. As you walk, you feel a sense of peace and tranquility wash over you, and you realize that this garden is your sanctuary. You feel connected to the Earth and the natural energy surrounding you, and you know that this is where you belong.

This garden is a manifestation of your love for witchcraft and the natural world. It's a space where you can practice your craft and connect with the energy of the Earth. But creating a magickal garden can be a daunting task, and you might be wondering where to begin.

Perhaps you've struggled with finding the right plants to use in your spells or have had trouble growing them. Maybe you've had difficulty creating a space that feels both functional and mystical. You might have even experienced a lack of motivation to start your garden because it seems overwhelming.

I understand these struggles and pains, but I'm here to tell you that it doesn't have to be so difficult. With the right knowledge and guidance, you can infuse witchcraft into your garden effectively and create a space that is not only beautiful but also functional.

You may think that the catalyst that brought you to this book is a desire to start a garden, but it's a burning desire to deepen your connection to nature and your own personal witchcraft journey. You want to create a space that allows you to harness the natural energy of the Earth and use it to fuel your spells and rituals.

If you also want to expand your knowledge of green witchcraft, then why not research this magickal path in the companion to this book *"Discover Your Green Witch Path"*? Using this companion book, you can learn and develop meditation skills, spellwork and grounding techniques before embarking on a journey to grow your own magickal garden.

But before we dive into the details of this book, let's talk about you. You've always felt a connection to nature and the magick that flows through it. You've been drawn to the idea of witchcraft for as long as you can remember and have recently decided to take the leap and start your witchy garden. You can't wait to create a space that's infused with your energy and the energy of the Earth.

But as you sit down to plan your garden, you realize that you don't quite know where to start. You don't know which plants to choose, how to arrange them, or how to infuse them with magick. You're worried that you'll mess something up or that your garden won't turn out the way you want it to.

In this book, you'll find everything you need to know to create a garden that's both beautiful and magickal. I'll share with you the problems and pain I experienced in the beginning when I started my witchy garden. You'll learn how to use my Green Witch Garden Formula, which is like a spell for creating a magickal garden. This formula is the result of years of research and experimentation, and it's been tested by countless gardeners who have achieved amazing results.

By reading this book, you'll get all the shortcuts you need to create your magickal garden without having to go through the trial and error that I did. You'll learn which plants to choose, how to arrange them, and how to infuse them with magick. You'll also discover the benefits of having a magickal garden, such as a deeper connection to nature, a sense of peace and tranquility, and the ability to use your garden for spellwork and rejuvenation.

Imagine yourself walking through a sprawling garden, surrounded by the fragrant scents of lavender, rosemary, and chamomile. The sun is warm on your face, and the soft rustling of leaves and grasses fills your ears. You feel the energy of the Earth flowing through your body, connecting you to the magickal world around you. This is the kind of experience you can have with your magickal garden.

This book is the culmination of all the knowledge I've accumulated over the years. But my knowledge and techniques aren't new. They build on the same traditions of herbalist witches from days of yore. In this book, my goal is to provide you with a step-by-step guide that will help you design, plant, and use your magickal garden. I want to give you the shortcuts I've learned over the years so that you don't have to spend years figuring it out on your own. So, let's get started!

# CHAPTER I

# WHAT IS GREEN WITCHCRAFT?

I n this chapter, we'll be exploring the world of green witchcraft and what it means to be a green witch.

Green witchcraft has its roots in ancient traditions of nature worship, and it is believed to have originated in Europe during the Middle Ages. In those times, people looked to nature and the cycles of the seasons for guidance and inspiration. They saw the world around them as a reflection of the divine, and they believed that by connecting with nature, they could tap into its power and wisdom.

As time went on, green witchcraft evolved and adapted to new cultures and beliefs. Today, it is a modern practice that combines elements of herbalism, magick, and spirituality. At its core, green witchcraft is about forming a deep connection with the natural world, and using that connection to enhance your life and the lives of those around you.

You believe in the power of nature to heal, guide, and inspire. You see plants, animals, and the elements as living beings with their energy and consciousness. You use herbs and other natural materials to create spells and potions that harness this energy and direct it toward your goals.

Being a green witch is all about being in tune with the rhythms of nature, and living in harmony with the world around you. It's about relying on your intuition and your bond with nature to inform your decisions and behavior. It involves nurturing a deep appreciation and respect for the intricate and captivating aspects of the natural environment.

But first, take a moment to reflect on what it means to you to be a green witch. How do you connect with the natural world, and what draws you to this practice? Think about these questions as we continue our journey together.

## WHAT IS A GREEN WITCH?

Have you ever heard of green witchcraft? It's a fascinating and nature-focused practice that works with the energies of nature to create balance and harmony in your life. It's all about having a dialogue with nature and using the cycles of the moon to guide your spiritual practices.

One of the most unique aspects of green witchcraft is its use of herbs. Green witches often have extensive knowledge of herbalism and use it in their spells, potions, and rituals. They understand the healing and magickal properties of plants and use them to harness the power of nature.

Nature-relatedness is another hallmark of green witchcraft. Green witches have a deep connection to the natural world and see the interconnectedness of all things. They believe in the importance of respecting and preserving the environment and often incorporate eco-friendly practices into their daily lives.

Green witches also focus on balancing and grounding energy. They understand that everything in the world has energy and that it's important to keep that energy in balance. Through practices such as meditation and grounding exercises, green witches seek to find harmony and peace within themselves and the world around them.

A naturalistic worldview is at the heart of green witchcraft. Green witches believe in the power of nature and see the divine in all things. They often practice their craft in outdoor settings, such as forests or gardens, and feel a deep spiritual connection to the natural world.

So, if you're drawn to nature and the power of the Earth, green witchcraft might be the perfect spiritual practice for you. With its focus on herbs, nature-relatedness, energy balance, and a naturalistic worldview, it's a beautiful and meaningful way to connect with the world around you.

### *The Defining Values of a Green Witch*

One of the most unique aspects of green witchcraft is that there are no set rules of conduct. Instead, you are encouraged to follow your intuition and use your inner compass to guide your actions. This allows for flexibility and creativity in your spiritual practice, as you can tailor it to fit your individual needs.

Another defining value of green witchcraft is the idea that green witches are caregivers and guardians of harmony. This means that you strive to maintain balance and harmony in all aspects of your life, including your relationships with others and the natural world. You seek to live in harmony with the Earth and all of its creatures and work to protect and preserve the environment.

Green witches are also observers of both left- and right-handed paths. The left-handed path is often associated with darkness and black magic, while the right-handed path is associated with light and white magic. As a green witch, you recognize the existence of both paths and strive to find a balance between them. You may encounter both types of energies in your practice, but you always work with the intention of maintaining balance and harmony.

Compassion combined with critical thought is another important value of green witchcraft. You approach your spiritual practice with an open heart and a desire to help others, but you also use critical thinking and discernment to ensure that your actions are ethical and in alignment with your values. You understand the importance of compassion and empathy but also recognize the need for personal responsibility and accountability. Recognizing these needs and wanting to nurture and protect all living beings is not always enough to make an informed decision.

That's why combining your compassion with critical thought is essential. It means taking the time to consider all the angles of a situation and weighing the potential outcomes. It involves examining your own biases and assumptions and being open to new information and perspectives.

It's important to remember that critical thought does not diminish your compassion. Rather, it helps you to make the most effective and compassionate choices. By approaching situations with both empathy and logic, you can create solutions that benefit both the individual and the collective.

Remember that it's okay to take your time and consider all the information before making a decision. Your commitment to both compassion and critical thought is a valuable asset to your green witch practice and to the world around you.

Keep up the good work, and continue to cultivate both. You possess the ability to create a beneficial influence on the world.

In essence, the defining values of green witchcraft revolve around living in harmony with the natural world, embracing creativity and individuality, and maintaining balance and compassion in all aspects of your life. By embracing these values, you can cultivate a meaningful and fulfilling spiritual practice that resonates with your unique spirit and personality.

## THE DIFFERENCE BETWEEN GREEN WITCHES AND OTHER WITCHES

You may already know that being a witch is a diverse and multifaceted practice, and there are actually a myriad of different types of witches. It's important to remember that each type of witchcraft is unique and has its own set of beliefs, practices, and traditions.

As a green witch, you use your connection with the natural world to enhance your magic and spiritual practices. You may work with herbs and other natural elements, such as crystals, to create spells and rituals that align with the rhythms of nature.

But it's important to understand that green witches are just one type of witch among many. There are witches who practice divination, such as Tarot and astrology, and witches who specialize in kitchen magic, healing magic, and more.

As you explore witchcraft, you may find that you resonate more with one type of witchcraft over another. It's all about finding what works best for you and your unique path. Don't feel like you have to conform to a specific type of witchcraft in order to be a "real" witch. Your individual journey is what matters most.

Keep an open mind as you continue to learn about the different types of witches and witchcraft. Each type of witchcraft has something valuable to offer, and you may find that incorporating elements from different traditions into your practice can enrich your spiritual journey.

Remember, there's no right or wrong way to be a witch. Embrace your unique path, and don't be afraid to try new things as you continue to grow and evolve as a witch.

### *What About White Witches and Hedge Witches?*

As you continue to explore the world of witchcraft, you may come across terms like "white witch" and "hedge witch." While there are similarities between these types of witches and green witches, there are also some key differences you need to recognize.

White witches are practitioners of witchcraft who focus on the use of "white magick" which is often associated with positivity, healing, and protection. They seek to use their magick for good and to benefit others, rather than for personal gain or harm to others.

White witches may use a variety of tools in their practice, including crystals, candles, herbs, and other natural elements. They may also incorporate ritual and ceremony into their practice and may work with specific deities or spirits.

Some white witches may also be skilled in divination, like Tarot or astrology, and may use these tools to gain insight into themselves and the world around them. They might also work with energy, such as the use of Reiki or other kinds of energy healing. While white witches also have a focus on healing and protection, their magick is rooted in the natural world and the energy of the Earth. Green witches often work with herbs, plants, and other natural elements to enhance their magick, whereas white witches may use a variety of tools such as crystals, candles, and charms.

On the other hand, hedge witches are similar to green witches in that they also have a deep connection to nature, but their focus is more on the boundaries between worlds. Hedge witches are practitioners of witchcraft who have a strong connection to nature and the natural world. They are often skilled in working with herbs and other natural elements and may incorporate these elements into their magick and healing practices.

The term "hedge" refers to the boundary between the physical world and the spiritual world. Hedge witches are known for their ability to navigate the peripheral spaces between worlds, and may use their magick to facilitate communication and understanding between different realms. They may also be involved in dream work and lucid dreaming and may use these practices to gain wisdom and insight into themselves and the world around them.

Hedge witches are often skilled in divination and astral projection, and may work with spirits and other entities. While green witches may incorporate elements of divination and spirit work into their practice, their primary focus is on working with the natural world and its energies.

## SIGNS YOU'RE A GREEN WITCH

If you find yourself drawn to the beauty and power of the natural world, you may have the potential to be a green witch. Here are some signs that suggest you may have a connection to this particular path:

- You enjoy making your own ritual tools from natural objects, such as stones, feathers, and herbs. You appreciate the energy and history of these items and enjoy crafting them into something that is unique and meaningful to you.
- You are passionate about animal and/or environmental activism and seek to make a

positive impact on the world around you. You recognize the interconnectedness of all living things and strive to live in harmony with nature.

- You are focused on spreading awareness of ethically sourced materials and making a conscious effort to support sustainable and eco-friendly products. You care about the impact your actions have on the environment and on other people.
- You work with Animal Guides and Plant Spirits and feel a deep connection to these energies. You may use meditation, visualization, or other techniques to communicate with these entities and learn from them.
- You love spending time hiking, exploring parks and gardens, and immersing yourself in nature. You feel a sense of peace and fulfillment when you are surrounded by natural beauty.
- You are attuned to nature's cycles and rhythms and may feel a sense of connection to the changing seasons, lunar cycles, or other natural phenomena. You may use this awareness in your magickal practice and may celebrate seasonal holidays or perform rituals during certain lunar phases.

- You feel a collective of plant energy and are aware of the interconnectedness of all living things. You may use this awareness to cultivate a deeper sense of empathy and compassion for others.
- You converse with plants and animals and may feel a sense of kinship with them. You may enjoy talking to your plants or leaving offerings for the animals that visit your home or garden.
- You have a deep reverence for nature and recognize its power and beauty. You may incorporate this reverence into your magickal practice and may seek to honor and protect the natural world in all that you do.

Remember, being a green witch is a personal journey and a unique expression of your individual spirituality. If these signs resonate with you, don't be afraid to explore this path further and see where it takes you.

Here are three summary points for you:

1. Green witchcraft is a practice that emphasizes the use of natural materials and a deep connection to the Earth and its cycles. As a green witch, you may work with plants, herbs, and other natural elements to create spells, potions, and rituals.

2. In green witchcraft, there is a strong focus on the balance between light and dark, and the interconnectedness of all things.

3. As you explore the path of green witchcraft, it's important to remember that there is no "right" or "wrong" way to practice. You may find that certain practices or tools resonate with you more than others, and that's okay. Ultimately, the most important thing is to cultivate a deep connection to the natural world and to approach your practice with an open heart and mind.

Now, let's dive deeper into the topic of the Green Witch Garden Formula in the next chapter. As a green witch, you may find that creating and tending to a garden is an important aspect of your practice. In this chapter, you'll learn how to create a magickal garden that reflects your connection to nature and supports your spellwork. The Green Witch Garden Formula offers guidance on selecting plants, designing your garden, and incorporating magickal elements like crystals, statues, and candles. With this knowledge, you'll be able to create a garden that not only enhances your magickal practice but also provides a peaceful and grounding space for you to connect with the natural world. So get ready to get your hands dirty and create a magickal garden that will nourish your body, mind, and spirit!

# CHAPTER 2
# THE GREEN WITCH GARDEN FORMULA

*"The garden suggests there might be a place where we can meet nature halfway."*

— MICHAEL POLLAN

I f you're a green witch, you already know how important it is to connect with the natural world and draw on its energy for your magickal practice. And one of the best ways to do that is by creating a magickal garden. However, designing a garden that is both beautiful and practical for your magickal work can be a bit overwhelming. That's where the Green Witch Garden Formula comes in.

In this chapter, you'll learn the essential aspects and stages of planning and designing a magickal garden.

You'll discover how to select the right plants for your garden, based on their magickal properties and correspondences. You'll also learn how to design your garden to reflect your own unique style and energy, and how to incorporate magickal elements like statues, candles, and crystals.

Think of the Green Witch Garden Formula as a special recipe that you can use to create a garden that is in harmony with nature's energy and your own magickal practice. With this formula, you'll be able to create a garden that not only supports your spellwork but also provides a peaceful and inspiring space for you to connect with the natural world. So let's get started and unlock the secrets of creating a truly magickal garden!

## HOW TO PLAN YOUR GREEN WITCH GARDEN

Planning a green witch garden can seem like a daunting task, but with the 6 steps of the Green Witch Garden Formula, you can create a beautiful and magickal garden that reflects your connection to the Earth.

### 1. Choosing the Right Location

Choosing the right location is one of the first things you need to do for your garden. Here are some steps to help you get started:

- **Consider the amount of sunlight:** Most herbs and plants require at least 6 hours of sunlight each day, so it's important to choose a location that gets plenty of natural light.
- **Check the soil availability:** Make sure that the soil in your chosen location is suitable for growing the plants you want to include in your garden. If the soil is too sandy or too heavy, you may need to amend it before planting.
- **Think about the location on your property:** Consider the layout of your property and choose a location for your garden that is easily accessible and visible. If you plan to use your garden for meditation or ritual work, you may want to choose a more secluded spot.
- **Access for watering:** Make sure your garden is located near a water source so you can easily water your plants. You may also want to consider installing a rain barrel to collect rainwater.
- **Consider the climate of your local area:** Be sure to choose plants that are well-suited to your local climate. If you live in a region with cold winters, you may need to choose plants that can survive the colder temperatures.

By taking these factors into consideration, you can choose the perfect location for your green witch garden. Remember, every garden is unique, so don't be afraid to experiment and make it your own.

### 2. Including Spirits in Your Planning

When it comes to planning a green witch garden, it's not just about finding the right physical location. You also want to make sure that the energy of the place is in alignment with your intentions for the garden. That's where the spirits of the place come in.

As a green witch, you have a deep connection to the natural world and the spirits that inhabit it. When planning your garden, take the time to tune into the energy of your property and seek out the help of the spirits of the place to find an ideal site. You may want to meditate or perform a ritual to connect with these spirits and ask for their guidance.

When selecting a location for your garden, focus on finding a spot that feels good both physically and spiritually. Look for an area that is already alive with natural energy and feels welcoming to you. You may also want to consider the energies associated with the cardinal directions and align your garden accordingly.

When it comes to the cardinal directions, there are four main points to keep in mind.

- First, there's the North, which represents stability, grounding, and wisdom. This direction is often associated with the element of Earth.
- Next, there's the East, which represents new beginnings, creativity, and inspiration. This direction is often associated with the element of Air.
- Third, there's the South, which represents passion, energy, and transformation. This direction is often associated with the element of Fire.
- Last, there's the West, which represents introspection, emotions, and intuition. This direction is often associated with the element of Water.

By considering these energies, you can align your garden in a way that supports your intentions and creates a harmonious environment for growth and abundance.

### 3. Map Your Space

Now that you have chosen the perfect location for your green witch garden, it's time to map out the space. This will help you visualize the layout of your garden and ensure that you have enough room for all of the plants you want to include.

Start by replicating the site you've chosen on paper. You can use a simple pencil and paper or try a digital tool like Garden Planner to create a more detailed layout. Be sure to include any existing features, such as trees or shrubs, that you want to keep in your garden design.

Mapping out your garden space will also help you determine the size of the beds and the spacing between plants. This is important because overcrowding can lead to poor growth and disease. It is crucial to bear in mind the size and shape of a mature plant. You must allow your plants room to grow fully to avoid the need for moving them to different areas of your garden.

Remember, mapping out your garden space is not just about practicality. It's also a chance to express your creativity and vision for your garden. Consider incorporating winding paths, hidden nooks, or special areas for meditation or ritual work.

### 4. What Type of Witchy Garden Are You Planning?

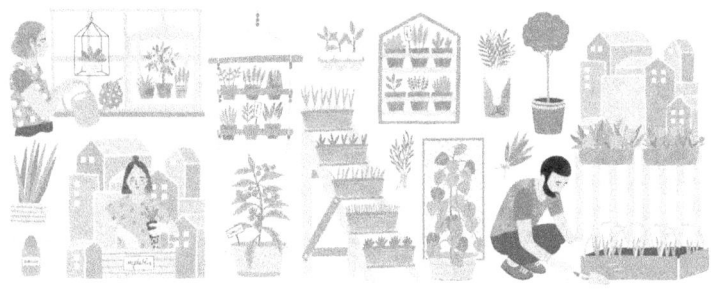

When it comes to planning your green witch garden, you have so many options to choose from! There are many different types of witchy gardens that you can create, each with its own unique energy and purpose.

Some popular types of witchy gardens include the moon garden, elemental garden, fire garden, water garden, Earth garden, air garden, astrological garden, and medicinal herb garden. Each of these gardens focuses on a different aspect of nature and can be tailored to your own personal style and intentions.

To decide on what type of witchy garden you want, think about what energies you want to bring into your space. Are you drawn to the calming energy of water, the fiery energy of the sun, or the grounding energy of the Earth? Do you want to focus on astrological correspondences or medicinal herbs for healing?

Once you've decided on a theme for your garden, you can start selecting plants and design elements that align with your intentions. For example, if you're creating a moon garden, you may want to include plants that bloom at night and incorporate silver or white elements into your design.

### 5. Choosing Your Shrines and Guardians

Incorporating shrines and guardians into your green witch garden can help you connect more deeply with the natural world and create a sacred space for your practice. There are many different types of statues, garden art, and other objects that you can use to bring a sense of magick and intention to your garden.

One way to incorporate guardians into your garden is by choosing statues or garden art that resonates with you. For example, you may want to include a statue of a goddess or a fairy to represent the feminine energy of the natural world. Or, you may want to include a totem animal that represents strength and protection.

Shrines are a fantastic way to honor and connect with the spirits of your garden. You can create a small altar or shrine using stones, shells, or other natural objects, and leave offerings of herbs, flowers, or other items that are meaningful to you. You may also want to include a mirror in your shrine to reflect the beauty of your garden and invite positive energy into your space.

### 6. Choosing Your Plants

Choosing the right plants for your green witch garden is an essential part of the design process. Plants have their own unique energies and properties, so it's important to select plants that align with your intentions and goals for your garden.

Start by creating a wish list of all the plants you want to include in your garden. This list can include herbs, flowers, and other plants that you feel drawn to. As you're creating your list, consider the properties of each plant and how they align with your goals for your garden. For example, if you want to create a garden that promotes healing, you may want to include plants like lavender or chamomile, which are known for their calming and soothing properties.

When selecting plants for your garden, it's also crucial to consider the climate and growing conditions in your location. Choose plants that are well-suited to your local climate and will thrive in the soil and light conditions of your garden.

Choose plants that resonate with you and align with your intentions and goals for your garden. By selecting the right plants, you can create a beautiful and magickal space that enhances your connection to the natural world and supports your spiritual practice.

## INDOOR GARDEN DESIGNS

If you don't have an outdoor space for your green witch garden or you simply want to bring some of that energy indoors, an indoor garden is a great option. There are many different types of indoor garden designs to choose from, each with their own unique look and feel.

One popular indoor garden design is the windowsill garden. This design involves using a windowsill as a base for your plants, usually in small containers or a planter box. To create a windowsill garden, you'll need some small pots, potting soil, and of course, your chosen plants. This type of indoor garden is perfect for those who have limited space and want to add some greenery to their living space.

Another popular indoor garden design is the hanging planter. This design involves hanging plants from the ceiling or a wall, using baskets or other hanging containers. You can use a variety of plants for this type of indoor garden, including trailing vines and small herbs. To set up a hanging planter, you'll need hanging baskets or containers, potting soil, and hooks or brackets to hang them.

If you want an indoor garden that you can move around your home as needed, consider creating a portable indoor garden. This design involves using a planter box with wheels or a small cart to hold your plants. You can use a variety of plants for this type of indoor garden, including herbs and small vegetables.

Stackable planters are another great option for indoor gardens. These planters consist of several tiers of containers stacked on top of each other, allowing you to grow a variety of plants in a small space. To set up a stackable planter, you'll need several tiers of containers, potting soil, and your chosen plants.

Finally, you can create a big pot planter for your indoor garden. This design involves using a large pot to hold several different plants. You can mix and match different herbs, flowers, and other plants to create a beautiful and unique indoor garden. To set up a big pot planter, you'll need a large pot, potting soil, and your chosen plants.

### Indoor Gardening Tips

Indoor gardening can be a great way to connect with nature and have fresh herbs on hand for cooking or spellwork. Here are some helpful hints to get started:

- **Provide strong light:** Indoor plants need plenty of light to grow, so make sure they're placed near a sunny window or under grow lights.
- **Keep the temperature at around 65–70 degrees Fahrenheit (18–21 degrees Celsius):** Most herbs prefer temperatures in this range, so try to keep your indoor garden at an herbal comfy temperature.
- **Allow for good air circulation:** This can help prevent unwanted mold or mildew from developing in your pots. You can use a small fan or crack a window to keep the air moving.

- **Pick appropriate pots for your herbs:** Make sure your pots are the right size for your herbs, and choose a material that allows for good drainage. You may also want to consider the design of your pots to fit with the aesthetic of your indoor garden.
- **Choose the right soil:** Use a well-draining soil mix that is formulated for indoor plants to ensure your herbs have the nutrients they need to grow.

With these tips, you'll be on your way to enjoying a thriving indoor garden in no time!

## OUTDOOR GARDEN DESIGNS

Now let's explore some outdoor garden designs that you can try out. These designs will help you get started with your outdoor garden setup.

- A tabletop planter is a great option for small spaces, and it involves planting herbs in small pots on a tabletop or on a shelf. You can use small pots and arrange them in a creative pattern.
- Hanging baskets are perfect for growing herbs that can trail down from the baskets. You can

hang these baskets on a wall, balcony, or even from a tree.

- Planting herbs with other crops can be an excellent way to maximize your garden space. You can plant herbs between your vegetable crops or in the borders of your flower beds.
- Raised herb garden beds can be built in any shape or size, depending on the available space. You can use wood or stone to create raised beds and fill them with the appropriate soil mix.
- A dedicated herb garden planter involves planting herbs in a large container or planter that is exclusively reserved for herbs. You can add some garden art or statues to make it more aesthetically pleasing.
- Vertical gardening is a wonderful way to utilize your garden walls or fences to grow herbs. You can install shelves, a trellis, or use a vertical garden kit to get started.
- A tiered herb garden involves planting herbs on different levels or tiers. Wooden or metal-tiered stands are great for holding pots.

Remember to choose the design that suits your needs and preferences, and consider the materials and location when setting up your outdoor garden.

*Outdoor Gardening Tips*

Here are some tips for planting outdoor herb gardens:

- **Pay attention to where you're planting:** Different herbs have different sun and soil preferences. Be sure to choose a location that matches the needs of your specific herbs.
- **Outdoor herbs may require more frequent watering:** Plants outdoors may require more watering than indoor plants, especially during hot and dry weather. Make sure to water your herbs regularly to keep the soil consistently moist.
- **Organic fertilizers and natural pest-control methods are essential:** Avoid using synthetic fertilizers and pesticides in your outdoor herb garden. Instead, choose organic fertilizers and natural pest-control methods, like using insect-repelling plants or companion planting strategies.
- **Bolting can alter the flavor of some herbs:** Bolting occurs when herbs start to produce flowers and seeds, which can affect the flavor of the leaves. To prevent bolting, make sure your plants are getting enough water and aren't

getting too hot or stressed. You can also trim back the flowers and buds as they appear.

## PATIO GARDEN DESIGNS

Creating a beautiful and functional garden on your patio or balcony can be a fun and rewarding experience. Here are some ideas to get you started:

- **Pick planters based on visual appeal as well as water needs:** Choose containers that fit your space and style, but also make sure they are appropriate for the plants you want to grow. Consider factors like drainage and water retention when selecting your containers.
- **Keep lighting in mind:** Ensure your plants get the appropriate amount of light they need to grow. Some plants require more sun than others, so choose plants that are suited to the light conditions on your patio or balcony.
- **No need to worry as much about fertilizer:** Plants in beds tend to use up soil nutrients quickly, so it's important to fertilize regularly. However, since you are using containers, you don't have to worry as much about nutrients leaching into the surrounding soil, which means you can fertilize less often.

- **Remember the "thriller, filler, spiller" method if container planting:** Use tall plants (thrillers), mid-sized plants (fillers), and trailing plants (spillers) in your containers to create a visually appealing and balanced arrangement.

With these tips and a bit of creativity, you can create a beautiful and functional garden on your patio or balcony that will provide you with fresh herbs, vegetables, or flowers all season long.

Great job exploring different types of gardens and learning about the Green Witch Garden Formula! Here are three summary points to remember:

1. The Green Witch Garden Formula emphasizes the use of natural materials, organic methods, and intuition when planning and tending to your garden.
2. There are many different types of gardens you can create, both indoors and outdoors, including windowsill gardens, raised beds, patio gardens, and more.
3. No matter what type of garden you choose, it's important to pay attention to factors like lighting, temperature, air circulation, water needs, and soil quality to ensure your plants thrive. With these tips in mind, you're well on

your way to creating a beautiful and sustainable garden that nourishes both your body and soul.

Now that you have an idea of what to plant and how to care for them, it's time to gather the necessary tools and supplies to make your gardening experience a success. In the next chapter, you'll learn about the various gardening tools and supplies that are essential for creating and maintaining your own magikcal garden. Whether you're a beginner or an experienced gardener, understanding the tools and supplies needed will make the process more efficient and enjoyable. So, let's dive in and explore the world of gardening tools and supplies!

# CHAPTER 3
# GATHERING YOUR TOOLS AND SUPPLIES

As you continue your journey in creating your own green witch garden, it's important to have the right tools and supplies at your disposal. Just as other types of witches need their magickal tools, you will need your own set of gardening tools to help bring your sacred space to life.

In this chapter, we will explore the essential tools and supplies you will need to create a thriving garden, whether you're a beginner or an experienced gardener. With the right equipment and a little bit of knowledge, you can transform your outdoor or indoor space into a magickal oasis of plants and herbs. Let's get started!

## WHAT YOU'LL NEED TO GROW YOUR GARDEN

When it comes to growing your garden, there are a few essential tools that you will need to ensure your plants are happy and healthy. Here are some of the most important tools and supplies you will need:

- **Trowel:** A trowel is a small handheld tool that is essential for digging small holes, transplanting seedlings, and moving soil around your garden. A good trowel will have a sturdy metal blade and a comfortable grip.
- **Spade:** A spade is a relatively bigger tool that is perfect for digging large holes, breaking up soil, and moving larger amounts of soil. It is important to have a spade that is comfortable to use and made of high-quality materials.
- **Gardening knife:** A gardening knife is a versatile tool that can be used for everything from pruning plants to harvesting vegetables. It

is important to have a sharp, sturdy knife that is easy to hold and use.

- **Gloves:** Gardening gloves are important for protecting your hands while you work in your garden. They can also help to prevent blisters and keep your hands clean and dry.
- **Twine:** Twine is an essential tool for tying up plants and creating supports for climbing vegetables. It is important to choose a twine that is strong and durable, but also gentle on your plants.
- **Watering can/hose:** Keeping your plants well-watered is essential for their health and growth. A watering can or hose is necessary for getting water to your plants in a controlled and efficient manner.
- **Gardening apron:** A gardening apron can help to protect your clothes from dirt, mud, and other garden debris. Try to find a washable apron with plenty of pockets to hold all of your necessary tools.
- **Hoe:** A hoe is a versatile tool that can be used for everything from cultivating soil to removing weeds. It is important to choose a hoe that is comfortable to use and made of high-quality materials.

- **Pruning clippers:** Pruning clippers are essential for keeping your plants healthy and tidy. They can be used for everything from deadheading flowers to cutting back overgrown branches.
- **Spray bottle:** A spray bottle is a useful tool for misting your plants with water or other treatments. It is important to choose a bottle that is easy to use and made of durable materials.

By having these essential gardening tools and supplies, you will be well-equipped to start your own garden and watch it thrive.

## PICKING THE RIGHT CONTAINERS

Here are some tips for picking the right planters for your herbs based on different materials:

**Ceramic:**

- Ceramic pots are great for herbs that require consistent moisture, as they tend to retain moisture well.
- They come in a variety of colors and styles to match your decor.
- Be sure to choose a pot with a drainage hole to prevent water from accumulating and potentially causing root rot.

**Terra cotta:**

- Terra cotta pots are a classic choice for herb gardens, as they allow for airflow and drainage.
- They can be porous, which can cause them to dry out faster, so keep an eye on your soil moisture levels.
- You can paint or decorate terra cotta pots to match your personal style.

**Plastic:**

- Plastic pots are lightweight and affordable, making them a great option for beginners or for those who need to move their plants around frequently.
- They come in a range of sizes and colors.
- Look for pots with drainage holes, and consider using saucers underneath to catch excess water.

**Metal:**

- Metal planters can add a unique touch to your herb garden, and can come in a variety of colors and styles.
- They can heat up quickly in the sun, so be sure to choose a location that won't be too hot for your plants.
- Some metal pots may rust over time, so be sure to check the quality of the material before purchasing.

**Resin:**

- Resin pots are a durable and lightweight option that can mimic the look of natural materials like stone or wood.
- They come in a range of colors and designs.
- Look for pots with drainage holes, and consider adding rocks or gravel to the bottom to improve drainage.

Remember to consider your individual plant's needs when selecting a planter, and be sure to choose a size that will accommodate the plant's growth.

As a green witch, you may prefer natural materials when choosing pots for your plants because they align with your values of sustainability and connection to nature. Pots made from natural materials such as ceramic and terra cotta can be beneficial for plants, as they allow for proper drainage and airflow, and can regulate temperature and moisture levels. Additionally, natural materials can add an earthy and organic aesthetic to your garden, helping to create a more natural and harmonious environment. Using natural materials for your plant pots can also be a way to connect with the Earth and honor the natural cycles of growth and decay that are central to the practice of green witchcraft.

### Container Size

When it comes to choosing the right size container for your herbs, it's important to consider the size of their roots. You want to make sure that the pot is big enough to accommodate the roots while also leaving room for growth. Choosing a container that is too small can lead to cramped roots and hinder the plant's ability to absorb nutrients and water. On the other hand, choosing a pot that is too large can cause the soil to stay wet for too long, leading to root rot.

So, take the time to research each herb and determine the size of their roots. This information will help you choose the appropriate container size to ensure your herbs have ample room to grow and thrive. Remember, it's always better to choose a slightly larger pot than a smaller one to avoid stunting their growth. With the right size container, your herbs will be well on their way to becoming healthy, thriving plants!

### Drainage

When selecting pots or containers for your herbs, it's important to consider drainage. Proper drainage is necessary for healthy herb growth because it helps prevent root rot and other water-related issues.

You can look for pots with drainage holes or you can drill holes in the bottom of the pot yourself. Additionally, you can also add gravel or sand at the bottom of the container to aid in drainage.

When watering your herbs, ensure that you're not over-watering and that the excess water is draining out of the pot. By paying attention to drainage, you can help ensure that your herbs thrive and grow well in their new home.

### Consider Aesthetics

When picking planters for your herbs, you'll want to consider aesthetics as well. This is where you can get creative and choose pots that match your personal style and the overall vibe of your space. You can choose containers that match the colors of your balcony or patio, or select pots with unique shapes that add character to your garden.

For instance, if you have a minimalist decor, you might opt for simple white or neutral-colored pots. If you want to add a pop of color, you can choose pots in bright hues like blue or yellow. Alternatively, if you prefer a rustic look, you can go for terra cotta or wooden planters.

When selecting pots, you can also mix and match different colors and textures to create an eye-catching display. You can group different sizes and shapes of pots together, or choose one large statement planter to anchor your herb garden.

## PREPARING THE POTTING SOIL

When you're getting ready to plant your herbs, it's important to choose the right soil. While regular garden soil might seem like the obvious choice, it's actually not recommended for potted plants. Garden soil can become compacted, leading to poor drainage and oxygenation for the roots. A potting soil which is specially designed for use in containers is a great choice.

Potting soil is a mixture of materials that are meant to promote healthy root growth, including peat moss, perlite, vermiculite, and sometimes compost. It's formulated to provide good drainage while also retaining moisture and nutrients that the plants need to thrive.

Compost, on the other hand, is made up of decomposed organic matter, such as vegetable scraps and yard waste. While compost is a great way to enrich your garden soil, it's not typically used on its own as a planting medium. Instead, it's often added to potting soil or garden soil to improve the nutrient content.

When preparing your potting soil, it's important to follow the instructions on the bag and mix it thoroughly. You can also add in some extra perlite or vermiculite to increase drainage and aeration. By using the right soil, you'll set your herbs up for success and help them grow healthy and strong.

### The Soil Requirements for Herbs

When it comes to planting your herbs, it's important to consider the soil requirements to ensure that your herbs grow healthy and strong. One of the most important factors is the soil's ability to maintain moisture. Herbs typically require soil that is moist but not waterlogged.

Another important factor is the soil's nutrient content. Herbs need a good source of nutrients to thrive, and potting mixtures that contain compost or organic matter can be beneficial in providing these nutrients. You can also supplement your soil with fertilizers or other organic materials to ensure that your herbs get the nutrients they need. Just make sure that your organic materials don't contain any unpleasant odors like fish oil, especially when planting indoors. Although it may be good for the plants, it smells for weeks!

Lastly, the soil should be able to drain well to prevent root rot and other problems that can arise from water-logged soil. Mixing sand or grit into the potting mix can help with drainage, or you can place a layer of gravel at the bottom of your container before adding the soil. Overall, choosing the right soil is crucial in ensuring the success of your herb garden.

### *Preparing Soil for Herbs*

If you're planning to grow herbs outdoors in your yard, you'll need to prepare the soil to ensure that it's nutrient-rich and has good drainage. Here are some steps you can follow:

1. **Test the soil for moisture:** Before you start planting, make sure to test the soil to see if it's too dry or too wet. If it's too dry, water the soil before planting. If it's too wet, add some organic matter to improve drainage.
2. **Amend the soil:** If your soil lacks nutrients, you can amend it by adding organic matter

such as compost or well-rotted manure. This will help enrich the soil and promote healthy plant growth.

3. **Test the pH:** The ideal pH range for growing herbs is between 6 and 7. You can test the pH of your soil using a pH meter or test kit. If the pH is too low or too high, you can adjust it by adding lime or sulfur.

4. **Test for nutrient levels:** To ensure that your soil has enough nutrients, you can test it using a soil test kit. If the levels are low, you can add fertilizer or organic matter to boost them.

5. **Till and moisten the soil:** Once you've tested and amended the soil, use a tiller or garden fork to mix the soil and organic matter together. Make sure the soil is suitably moist but not waterlogged.

6. **Add soil to container beds/lots:** If you're planting in containers or raised beds, make sure to fill them with good quality potting soil that has good drainage and moisture retention.

By following these steps, you'll be able to prepare your soil properly and give your herbs the best chance to thrive.

## Planting Into Pots

If you're using pots, it's important to use a good potting mix that is specifically formulated for container gardening. You can either prepare the soil by following the steps outlined above and adding it to the pots, or you can make your own potting mix. A basic recipe for potting mix includes three parts peat moss or coco coir, one part compost, one part perlite, and one part manure or worm castings. This mix ensures that the soil is rich in nutrients and has good drainage.

If the soil in your area is sandy or has a lot of clay, you may need to add plenty of compost to provide enough nutrients for your herbs. You can also test the soil pH and nutrient levels to determine if you need to add any fertilizer. Once you have the soil ready, moisten it and add it to your pots or container beds.

Here are three important summary points to consider before planting your witchy garden:

1. Picking the right pots for your herbs is crucial. Consider the material, size, drainage, and aesthetics to ensure your plants thrive and look beautiful in their containers.
2. When it comes to soil requirements for herbs, it's important to choose a soil that can maintain moisture, has enough nutrients, and can drain well. Testing the soil, amending it with organic matter, and adding fertilizer if necessary can help ensure your herbs grow strong and healthy.
3. If you're growing herbs in pots, a potting mix recipe can be an excellent option. By combining peat moss or coco coir, compost, perlite, and

manure or worm castings, you can create a nutrient-rich soil that's perfect for your herbs. And if your soil is sandy or clay-heavy, adding plenty of compost can help provide the nutrients your plants need.

Now that you know how to prepare your soil and choose the right planter, you're ready to start selecting your herbs and plants. In the next chapter, we'll go over some helpful tips on how to choose the best herbs and plants for your garden. With the right knowledge and tools, you'll be on your way to growing a thriving herb garden in no time!

# CHAPTER 4
# PICKING WITCHY HERBS AND PLANTS

You may have heard the saying "knock on wood" when someone wants to avoid jinxing themselves. But did you know that the origins of this superstition date back to ancient times when people believed that spirits inhabited trees and knocking on the wood would awaken them for protection (Muckle, 2016)?

Just like the protective power of trees, many herbs and plants have been used for centuries in witchcraft for their magickal properties. And what better way to harness their power than by growing them in your own garden?

Planting herbs like lavender, sage, and rosemary not only adds beautiful scents and flavors to your home, but they also possess protective properties. Sage is known for its ability to clear negative energy, while rosemary is said to enhance memory and improve focus. And let's not forget the calming and relaxing effects of lavender, perfect for promoting peaceful sleep.

Other plants like chamomile and calendula are not only beautiful to look at, but they also have medicinal properties that have been used for centuries to soothe various ailments. And if you're looking for a plant to ward off evil spirits, consider planting a row of garlic, which has long been associated with protection and warding off evil.

So if you're looking to infuse some magick into your garden, consider planting these witchy herbs and plants. Who knows, maybe you'll even start knocking on wood for good luck too.

## PLANTS FOR ENERGETIC PROTECTION

Energetic protection refers to the use of plants and herbs in witchcraft to ward off negative energy, protect oneself from harm, and create a safe space. If you're looking to add some extra protection to your magickal practice, consider incorporating some of these powerful herbs into your garden.

**Peppermint:**

Peppermint is known for its refreshing scent and cooling properties, making it a popular ingredient in teas and essential oils. But did you know that peppermint can also be used in protection magic? It is said to repel negative energy and ward off evil spirits. Peppermint is easy to grow and thrives in full sun.

**Panax Ginseng:**

Panax Ginseng is a popular medicinal herb in traditional Chinese medicine, known for its ability to boost energy and immunity. It is also said to have protective properties, creating a barrier against negative energy and promoting clarity of thought. Panax Ginseng is commonly grown in Asia, but can also be found in the US and Canada.

## Chamomile:

Chamomile is known for its calming and soothing proper-ties, making it a popular ingredient in teas and beauty products. It is also believed to  have protective properties, promoting peaceful sleep and warding off negative energy. Chamomile enjoys growing in full sun.

## Mandrake Root:

Mandrake Root has a long history of use in witchcraft, associated with protection, fertility, and healing. It is said to possess powerful protec-tive energy, warding off evil  spirits and negative energy. Mandrake Root is commonly grown in Europe and Asia.

## Sage:

Sage is one of the most popular herbs in protection magic, known for its ability to cleanse negative energy and promote healing. It is also said to have the power to ward off evil spirits and protect against harm. Sage grows best in full sun.

**Bay Leaves:**

Bay leaves are a common ingredient in cooking, but they are also believed to possess protective properties. Bay leaves are said to promote clarity of thought, ward off negative energy, and protect against harm. Bay leaves can be grown in full sun or partial shade.

**Mugwort:**

Mugwort is a powerful herb used in protection magick, associated with warding off negative energy and promoting lucid dreaming. It is also believed to have the power to protect against psychic attacks and evil spirits. Mugwort can be easily grown in full sun or partial shade but not full shade.

## St. John's Wort:

St. John's Wort is a popular medicinal herb known for its ability to alleviate depression and anxiety. It is also said to have protective properties, creating a barrier against negative energy and promoting spiritual clarity. St. John's Wort can be grown in partial shade or full sun but not full shade.

## Myrrh:

Myrrh is a resinous herb with a long history of use in spiritual and religious ceremonies. It is believed to have protective properties, warding off negative energy and promoting healing. Myrrh enjoys growing in full sun or partial shade.

## Rue:

Rue is a powerful herb used in protection magic, associated with warding off evil spirits and negativity. It is also said to have the power to promote mental clarity and focus. Rue grows well in full sun or partial shade.

**Wormwood:**

Wormwood is a powerful herb used in protection magic, associated with warding off evil spirits and promoting psychic clarity. It is also believed to have the power to protect against harm and negative energy. Wormwood thrives in both full sun or partial shade.

**Angelica:**

Angelica is a versatile herb used in protection magic, associated with warding off negative energy and promoting healing. It is also said to have the power to promote spiritual clarity and protection. Angelica grows very well in full sun or partial shade.

**Hyssop:**

Hyssop is a powerful herb used in protection magic, associated with warding off negativity and promoting spiritual cleansing. It is also believed to have the power to promote mental clarity and focus. Hyssop grows easily in both full sun or partial shade.

**Thyme:**

Thyme is a popular culinary herb with a long history of use in medicine and magick. It is believed to have protective properties, creating a barrier against negative energy and promoting physical and emotional healing. Thyme is easy to grow and thrives in full sun.

**Horsetail:**

Horsetail is a unique herb with a long history of use in medicine and magick. It is said to possess protective properties, promoting physical and emotional healing and warding off negative energy. Horsetail thrives in full sun or partial shade.

**Comfrey:**

Comfrey is a versatile herb used in protection magic, associated with warding off negativity and promoting physical and emotional healing. It is also believed to have the power to promote spiritual clarity and protection. Comfrey does well in full sun or partial shade.

**Nettle:**

Nettle is a powerful herb used in protection magic, associated with warding off evil spirits and negativity. It is also said to have the power to promote physical and emotional healing and protect against harm. Nettle grows very easily in full sun or partial shade.

## PLANTS FOR GRIEF, TRAUMA, AND ANXIETY

Herbs have long been used in emotional healing, helping to soothe the mind and ease feelings of grief, trauma, and anxiety. These plants contain powerful medicinal and magickal properties that can help to uplift the spirit, promote relaxation, and ease the emotional burden that comes with challenging times.

**Rosemary:**

Rosemary is a popular herb with a rich history of use in medicine and magick. It is believed to have the power to promote mental clarity, improve memory, and ease feelings of grief and anxiety. Rosemary thrives in full sun and does exceptionally well in well-drained soil.

**Lemon Balm:**

Lemon Balm is a calming herb that can help to ease feelings of anxiety and promote relaxation. It is also said to have the power to uplift the spirit and ease feelings of grief.

Lemon balm can be grown easily in both full sun or partial shade.

**Roses:**

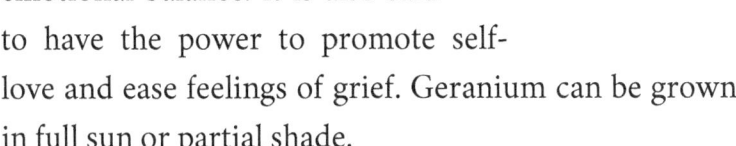

Roses are known for their beauty and sweet fragrance, but they are also a powerful herb used in emotional healing. Roses are believed to have the power to promote self-love, ease feelings of grief, and uplift the spirit. Roses grow very well in full sun and well-drained soil.

**Geranium:**

Geranium is a popular herb used in emotional healing, associated with easing feelings of anxiety and promoting emotional balance. It is also said to have the power to promote self-love and ease feelings of grief. Geranium can be grown in full sun or partial shade.

## Hibiscus:

Hibiscus is a beautiful flowering plant with a long
history of use in medicine
and magick. It is believed to
have the power to ease feelings
of anxiety, promote relaxation, and
uplift the spirit. Hibiscus is easy to grow in full sun and
well-drained soil.

## Lavender:

Lavender is a beloved herb
used in emotional healing,
known for its calming and
soothing properties. It is also
said to have the power to
promote relaxation, ease feelings of
grief, and uplift the spirit. Lavender can be grown in
either full sun or partial shade and does equally well in
both.

## Lemon:

Lemon is a powerful herb
used in emotional healing,
associated with easing feelings of anxiety and promoting
emotional balance. It is also said

to have the power to uplift the spirit and ease feelings of grief. Lemon trees require full sun and well-drained soil.

## Valerian:

Valerian is a calming herb used in emotional healing, associated with easing feelings of anxiety and promoting relaxation. It is also said to have the power to promote emotional balance and ease feelings of grief. Valerian can be grown easily in either full sun or partial shade.

## Hops:

Hops are a popular herb used in emotional healing, known for their calming and sedative properties. They are also believed to have the power to ease feelings of anxiety and promote relaxation. Hops grow very well in full sun or partial shade.

## Passionflower:

Passionflower is a powerful herb used in emotional healing, associated with easing feelings of anxiety and promoting relaxation. It is also said to have the power to uplift the spirit and ease feelings of grief. Passionflower enjoys growing in full sun or partial shade.

## Skullcap:

Skullcap is a calming herb used in emotional healing, associated with easing feelings of anxiety and promoting relaxation. It is also said to have the power to promote emotional balance and ease feelings of grief. Skullcap can be grown easily in either full sun or partial shade.

## PLANTS FOR PHYSICAL STRENGTH AND ENERGY

Herbs can play an important role in supporting physical health and energy. These plants contain a variety of compounds that can help with everything from reducing inflammation to increasing stamina. Let's explore some of the best herbs for physical strength and energy.

### Eleuthero:

Eleuthero is a type of ginseng that has been used for centuries to increase energy and reduce stress. It is also believed to enhance mental clarity and improve athletic performance. Eleuthero plants prefer partial shade to full sun and can grow in a variety of soil types. This herb is commonly grown in Asia and can be used in witchcraft to promote strength and endurance.

### Schisandra:

Schisandra is a berry that is native to China and Russia. It is known for its adaptogenic properties, which means that it can help the body respond to stress and increase energy levels. Schisandra plants prefer partial shade and well-draining soil. This herb is also believed to have anti-aging properties and is used in traditional Chinese medicine to promote longevity.

**Rhodiola Root:**

Rhodiola Root is another adaptogenic herb that is commonly used to increase stamina and reduce fatigue. It is believed to improve mental clarity and may also have antidepressant properties. Rhodiola plants prefer full sun and well-draining soil. This herb is commonly grown in colder regions such as Siberia and the Rocky Mountains and can be used in witchcraft to promote physical strength and endurance.

**Pseudostellaria Root:**

Pseudostellaria Root, also known as "false starwort," is a root vegetable that is commonly used in Chinese medicine. It is believed to have tonic properties that can help strengthen the body and increase endurance.

Pseudostellaria plants prefer partial shade and moist, well-draining soil. This herb is commonly grown in China and can be used in witchcraft to promote physical vitality.

**Holy Basil:**

Holy Basil, also known as "tulsi," is a plant that is native to India. It is known for its adaptogenic properties and is commonly used to reduce stress and increase energy levels. Holy Basil plants prefer full sun and well-draining soil. This herb is also believed to have anti-inflammatory and immune-boosting properties and can be used in witchcraft to promote physical well-being.

**Parsley:**

Parsley is a common herb that is used in many different cuisines. It is known for its high vitamin and mineral content, particularly vitamin C and iron. Parsley plants prefer partial shade and moist, well-draining soil. This herb is also believed to have diuretic properties and can be used in witchcraft to promote physical strength and vitality.

## Feverfew:

Feverfew is a plant that is native to Europe and has been used for centuries to treat headaches and other types of pain. It is also believed to have wonderful anti-inflammatory properties and may also help to boost the immune system. Feverfew plants prefer full sun to partial shade and well-draining soil. This herb is commonly grown in gardens and can be used in witchcraft to promote physical healing and strength.

## Chives:

Chives are a member of the onion family and are known for their high vitamin and mineral content, particularly vitamin C and iron. Chives plants prefer full sun and well-draining soil. They are also believed to have anti-inflammatory and immune-boosting properties and can be used in witchcraft to promote physical health and well-being.

**Oregano:**

Oregano is a common herb that is used in many different cuisines. It is known for its high antioxidant content and may also have anti-inflammatory properties. Oregano plants prefer full sun and well-draining soil. This herb is commonly grown in gardens and can be used in witchcraft to promote physical strength and vitality.

**Lemongrass:**

Lemongrass is a plant that is native to Southeast Asia and is commonly used in cooking. It is known for its high antioxidant content and may also have anti-inflammatory proper-ties. Lemongrass plants grow best in full sun and well-draining soil. This herb is commonly grown in gardens and can be used in witchcraft to promote physical strength and vitality.

Remember to always use caution when working with herbs, and consult with a qualified herbalist or health-care provider before eating or using any herbs for medicinal purposes.

## PICKING YOUR PLANTS AND HERBS

When it comes to choosing the herbs and plants for your garden, it's important to pick ones that you feel drawn to and have a natural connection with. The herbs you choose should also be ones that you can see yourself using in your craft. This ensures that you'll be more inclined to care for them and use them effectively in your practice. So, take some time to research and explore the different options, and trust your intuition when picking the ones that resonate with you the most.

### *Pick Plants and Herbs You Need*

When deciding which plants to include in your garden, it's important to think about the specific needs and goals you have in mind for your practice. Consider the different areas of your life where you could use some extra support, whether that be in emotional healing, energetic protection, physical strength, or spiritual connection. Once you've identified your needs, you can then begin researching which plants and herbs are best suited to help you achieve those goals.

For instance, if you're looking to bring more peace and calm into your life, herbs like lavender, chamomile, and lemon balm are great options. On the other hand, if you're looking to increase your energy levels and focus, herbs like ginseng, eleuthero, and rhodiola root may be more beneficial. If you're looking for spiritual connection, you might consider herbs like mugwort, wormwood, or frankincense.

Ultimately, by choosing plants and herbs that align with your specific needs and intentions, you'll be able to create a garden that not only supports your practice but also provides you with a sense of grounding and connection to the natural world.

### Consider the Seasons

Another important factor to consider when selecting plants for your garden is the timing of their maturity. To ensure a consistent supply of fresh herbs and plants, try to choose a diverse selection that matures at different times throughout the year.

For example, you might include some plants that mature in the spring, like parsley and chives, as well as some that mature in the summer, like lavender and lemon balm. In the fall, you could add in herbs like rosemary and thyme, and in the winter, you might focus on plants like sage and bay leaves.

By choosing a mix of herbs that mature at different seasons, you'll be able to enjoy a continuous supply of fresh herbs and plants throughout the year. Plus, this approach also helps to promote biodiversity in your garden and supports the natural rhythms of the Earth. So, take some time to research the different maturation times of the herbs you're interested in, and aim to create a diverse and well-rounded garden that can provide for you throughout the changing seasons.

Let's take a look at this table showing the maturation seasons for the different plants discussed previously in this chapter!

| Season | Spring | Summer | Autumn | Winter |
|---|---|---|---|---|
| **Type of Plant** | Chamomile<br>Sage<br>Myrrh<br>Comfrey<br>Nettle<br>Rosemary<br>Roses<br>Parsley<br>Chives | Chamomile<br>Peppermint<br>Panax Ginseng<br>Sage<br>Bay leaves<br>Mugwort<br>St. John's Wort<br>Rue<br>Wormwood<br>Angelica<br>Hyssop<br>Thyme<br>Horsetail<br>Comfrey<br>Nettle<br>Rosemary<br>Lemon Balm<br>Roses<br>Geranium<br>Hibiscus<br>Lavender<br>Lemon<br>Valerian<br>Hops<br>Passionflower<br>Skullcap<br>Eleuthero<br>Schisandra<br>Rhodiola Root<br>Pseudostellaria Root<br>Holy Basil<br>Parsley<br>Feverfew<br>Chives<br>Oregano<br>Lemongrass<br>Yarrow<br>Elderberry | Peppermint<br>Panax Ginseng<br>Mandrake Root<br>Bay leaves<br>Mugwort<br>St. John's Wort<br>Rue<br>Wormwood<br>Angelica<br>Hyssop<br>Thyme<br>Horsetail<br>Comfrey<br>Lemon Balm<br>Geranium<br>Hibiscus<br>Lavender<br>Lemon<br>Valerian<br>Hops<br>Passionflower<br>Skullcap<br>Eleuthero<br>Schisandra<br>Rhodiola Root<br>Pseudostellaria Root<br>Holy Basil<br>Feverfew<br>Oregano<br>Lemongrass<br>Yarrow<br>Elderberry | Mandrake Root<br>Myrrh |

## *Rosemary Is Great for Beginners*

If you're just starting out with a witchy herb garden, one great plant to consider is rosemary. This hardy herb is a popular choice for beginners because it's easy to grow and has a range of versatile uses in both culinary and magickal practices.

Rosemary is known for its aromatic and invigorating properties, which can help to promote mental clarity and improve focus. Additionally, it's believed to have protective properties that can help to ward off negative energy and promote healing. In some magickal traditions, rosemary is also associated with love and fidelity.

This herb is commonly grown in Mediterranean climates, but can be cultivated in a range of regions as long as it has access to well-draining soil and plenty of sunlight. It's a perennial plant that can thrive for several years with proper care, making it a great choice for a long-term addition to your garden.

Rosemary can be used in a variety of ways in your witchcraft practice, from burning as an incense to incorporating into spells and rituals. You can also incorporate it into your cooking and baking to infuse your meals with its unique flavor and magickal energy. Overall, rosemary is a versatile and beginner-friendly herb that can be a great starting point for anyone looking to cultivate their own witchy garden.

### Herbs Are Perfect for Baby Witches

If you're new to gardening and want to start growing plants for witchcraft, herbs are a great starting point. They are relatively easy to grow, and many have a long history of use in various forms of magick. Once you've become comfortable growing and caring for herbs, you can consider moving on to other types of plants, such as vegetables or flowers, that also have magickal properties.

When selecting plants to grow, choose ones that you feel drawn to or that have associations with the type of magick you want to practice. You may also want to consider growing a mix of plants that mature at different times of the year so that you always have fresh herbs to work with.

No matter which plants you choose to grow, remember to take the time to learn about their individual needs for soil, water, and sunlight. With a little bit of research and some care and attention, you can create a thriving witch garden that will nourish both your magickal practice and your body.

When choosing plants for your magickal garden, it's important to consider not only their symbolism and traditional uses but also their practicality for your location and gardening experience. You should choose plants that can thrive in your local climate and soil conditions and require the amount of care that you are able to provide.

Research the plants you are interested in and make sure they are safe for you, your family, and any pets that may be in your home. Additionally, consider the space you have available and how much room each plant will need to grow to maturity.

When selecting plants, keep in mind the specific purposes you want them to serve in your magickal practice. If you're looking for plants for protection or healing, consider options like lavender or chamomile. If you want to attract love or prosperity, look for plants like rose or basil.

Here are three of the most important points you should consider when deciding what plants to grow in your new magickal garden:

1. It is important to choose plants for your witchy garden that resonate with your personal intentions and magickal practice.

2. Consider the purposes of the plants, such as protection, emotional healing, physical strength, and energy, when making your selection.

3. For beginners, starting with herbs is a good option, and it is helpful to choose an assortment of plants that mature at different seasons.

Now that you have a better understanding of the types of plants to choose for your witchy garden, it's time to move on to the next step: Planting the garden. In the next chapter, you will learn how to prepare your garden bed, select the right tools, and get your plants in the ground. By following these tips and guidelines, you'll be well on your way to creating a thriving magickal garden that will serve as a source of inspiration and connection to the natural world. So roll up your sleeves and get ready to dig in!

# GUIDING ANOTHER WITCH TO THEIR MAGICKAL GARDEN

*"Love for life in all its forms is the basic ethic of witchcraft."*

— STARHAWK

As you know, a straight-up gardening book isn't all that helpful to the green witch. You might find guidance for two or three plants you're interested in, but the book's overall angle won't help you create the perfect magickal garden.

You picked up this book because you wanted specific guidance. You wanted to know how to work in tandem with nature and the moon to create a thriving garden from which you can create magickal remedies... and you found what you were looking for.

I'd like to take this opportunity to ask for your help in getting this guide out to more green witches – so they don't have to search for hours or cobble together an understanding by reading bits of regular gardening books and cross-referencing them with books on witchcraft and herbal remedies.

Don't worry – it won't keep you from your garden for long. In fact, it doesn't even require you to leave the couch – all it takes is a short review.

**By leaving a review of this book on Amazon, you'll show other green witches that everything they're looking for is contained in one book – and you'll show them exactly where they can find it.**

Simply by telling new readers how this book has helped you and what they'll find inside, you'll allow them to skip the long search process in finding guidance for planting a magickal garden and enjoying all its benefits.

Thank you so much for your support. Working in harmony with nature means working in harmony with each other too, and I'm so glad to have you on board.

**Scan the QR code below for a quick review!**

# CHAPTER 5

# PLANTING YOUR GARDEN

Now that you have picked out the perfect plants for your witchy garden, it's time to roll up your sleeves and get started with planting. In this chapter, we will cover the practical aspects of creating your garden, including soil preparation, planting techniques, and maintenance tips to keep your magickal garden thriving. So let's get started on this exciting journey of creating your own enchanting garden.

## HOW TO PLANT YOUR GARDEN

Here are the basic steps to plant your garden starting with seeds or seedlings:

1. **Choose a planting site:** Select a location that receives plenty of sunlight and has good soil drainage.
2. **Prepare the soil:** Loosen the soil and add organic matter like compost or aged manure to help provide nutrients. Work the soil with a garden fork or tiller.
3. **Decide whether to use seeds or seedlings:** Seeds can be more affordable but require more patience and care, while seedlings are easier to manage but may cost more.
4. **Sow herb seeds lightly:** Herbs like thyme, parsley, and basil should be sown lightly, as they only require a thin layer of soil to germinate.
5. **Keep soil evenly moist:** Water your seeds or seedlings regularly, making sure not to let the soil dry out or become too waterlogged.
6. **Ensure adequate drainage:** Make sure your planting containers or garden beds have adequate drainage to prevent water from pooling around the roots of your plants.

7. **Provide plenty of light:** Most herbs require at least 6 hours of sunlight per day, so make sure to choose a location that receives plenty of light. If you're starting your seeds indoors, you may need to use grow lights to provide adequate light.

8. **Check the seed packet for more information regarding timing:** Different herbs have different germination and growing times, so make sure to check the seed packet or do some research to ensure you're planting at the right time.

9. **Transplant seedlings:** Once your seedlings have grown enough to be transplanted, make sure to do so carefully to avoid damaging the delicate roots.

10. **Monitor and care for your plants:** Keep an eye on your plants for signs of pests, diseases, or nutrient deficiencies. Fertilize and prune as necessary.

*Tips for Seedlings*

Here are some tips on growing successful seedlings:

- **Check that seedlings have "true leaves":**
  Before transplanting your seedlings, make sure
  they have developed their first set of true
  leaves. These are the leaves that come after the
  initial cotyledons and look more like the leaves
  of the mature plant.
- **Water before transplanting:** Water your
  seedlings before transplanting them to help
  reduce stress and make it easier to remove them
  from their original container.

- **Fill in dirt in the new pot/container:** Fill the new container with fresh soil, leaving enough room at the top for the seedlings to be planted.

- **Remove seedlings from original pot:** Gently remove your seedlings from their original pot, taking care not to damage the roots. You can use a small trowel or spoon to scoop them out.

- **Plant in new container:** Dig a hole in the center of the new container and place the seedling in the hole, making sure the roots are covered with soil. Firm the soil around the base of the plant.

- **Water:** Water your newly transplanted seedlings to help settle them into their new home.

- **Place in shade, then move to sun:** After transplanting, it's best to place your seedlings in a shady location for a few days to help them adjust to their new environment. Then gradually move them to a sunnier location over the course of a week or so.

*Keep a Record of Your Plants*

The following are some things you may want to consider including in your plant record:

- **What it is:** Start by recording the name of the plant you're growing. You can also include any other identifying information, like the variety or cultivar (cultivated varieties).
- **Where you sowed the seeds:** Record where you planted your seeds or transplanted your seedlings, whether that's in a specific garden bed or container.
- **When to harvest:** Note when you should expect to be able to harvest your plant. This will vary depending on the type of plant, so make sure to do some research to find out the optimal harvesting time.
- **Magickal qualities:** If you're planting for the magickal or spiritual properties of plants, you may want to record any correspondences or associations with the plant you're growing. For example, lavender is associated with love and relaxation, while rosemary is associated with memory and protection.
- **Additional insights:** You may also want to record any additional insights or observations

you make about your plant over time. This could include things like how well it's growing, any pests or diseases it's experiencing, or any unexpected benefits or challenges you encounter.

Here is an example of a sample plant record for Lavender:

**What it is:** Lavender (Lavandula angustifolia), a fragrant herb that is commonly grown for its beautiful flowers and soothing scent.

**Where you sowed the seeds:** I planted the lavender seeds in a large container on my sunny balcony.

**When to harvest:** The optimal time for harvesting lavender is when the flowers are fully open but before they start to fade. I plan to harvest my lavender in mid-summer.

**Magickal qualities:** Lavender is associated with love, relaxation, and purification. I am growing it for its calming properties and plan to use it in my spiritual practice for meditation and self-care.

**Additional insights:** So far, my lavender plant is growing well and has a lovely scent. However, I have noticed some small insects on the leaves and will need to keep an eye on it to make sure it doesn't become infested with pests. Overall, I am excited to see how my lavender plant continues to grow and develop, and I am looking forward to harvesting its beautiful flowers.

### Annual, Biennial, and Perennial Herbs

Here's a quick breakdown of the differences between annual, biennial, and perennial herbs:

- **Annual herbs:** These are plants that complete their full life cycle in a single growing season. They grow from seed, produce leaves and flowers, and then die back in the fall or winter. Examples of annual herbs include dill, basil and cilantro.
- **Biennial herbs:** These are herbs that take two growing seasons to complete their life cycle. They grow from seed in the first season, produce foliage but no flowers, and then become dormant over the winter months. In the second season, they produce flowers and seeds before dying back. Examples of biennial herbs include angelica, parsley and caraway.
- **Perennial herbs:** These are herbs that live for multiple growing seasons. They may die back to the ground in the fall or winter, but they will regrow from their roots in the spring. Some

perennial herbs can live for many years or even decades. Examples of perennial herbs include thyme, sage, and lavender.

Understanding the differences between these three types of herbs can be helpful when planning your herb garden. For example, if you want to have fresh basil all season long, you'll need to plant new seeds or seedlings each year because basil is an annual herb. On the other hand, if you plant a perennial herb like thyme, you can enjoy fresh leaves year after year without needing to replant.

## THE IMPORTANCE OF COMPANION PLANTING

Companion planting is the practice of growing different plants in close proximity to one another for their mutual benefit. This can help to improve the health and productivity of your garden for many different reasons which will be covered in this next section.

## *The Benefits of Companion Planting*

Here are some key benefits of companion planting:

- **Crop protection:** Companion planting can help protect your crops from pests and diseases by repelling or distracting harmful insects, or by attracting beneficial insects that can help control pests. For example, planting marigolds alongside tomatoes can help repel nematodes, while planting dill or fennel near brassicas (plants in the cabbage family) can attract beneficial wasps that prey on cabbage worms.
- **Limiting risk to external elements:** Companion planting can help protect your crops from external elements like wind, sun, and heavy rain. For example, planting tall sunflowers or corn near your garden can help provide shade and protection from wind, while planting low-growing herbs like thyme or oregano can help protect the soil from erosion and runoff.
- **Positive hosting:** Companion planting can help create a positive hosting environment for beneficial insects like bees, butterflies, and hummingbirds. By planting flowers that these

pollinators are attracted to, you can help ensure that your garden is pollinated and productive.

- **Trap cropping:** Companion planting can also be used as a trap-cropping technique to lure pests away from your main crops. For example, planting sacrificial crops like radishes or nasturtiums near your vegetables can attract pests like flea beetles or aphids, which can then be removed or treated before they can do damage to your main crops.

By using companion planting in your garden, you can help create a more balanced and diverse ecosystem that is less susceptible to pests and diseases, and more resilient to external factors like weather and environmental changes.

### Factors to Consider

When planning your companion planting strategy, there are several factors to consider. These include the size, shape, and growth habits of the plants you're working with, as well as their nutrient and moisture requirements. You'll also want to consider any potential pest or disease issues, as well as any beneficial insects you'd like to attract.

**Growing conditions:** It's important to choose companion plants that have similar growing conditions to your main crops. These include factors like soil type, sun exposure, and water requirements. For example, if you're growing tomatoes in a sunny, well-drained area, you might want to consider planting basil, marigolds, or borage alongside them, as these plants all prefer similar growing conditions.

**Compatibility:** Not all plants are compatible with each other, and some combinations can actually be harmful. For example, planting beans alongside onions can actually inhibit the growth of the beans, while planting tomatoes near brassicas like cabbage or broccoli can attract pests like the cabbage worm. On the other hand, planting carrots alongside onions or leeks can help deter pests like carrot rust flies.

To ensure compatibility, it's important to thoroughly research your chosen plants to avoid planting those that are not compatible next to each other. You can also experiment with different combinations to see what works best in your garden.

By considering these factors and guidelines when planning your companion planting strategy, you can create a garden that is both beautiful and productive, while minimizing pest and disease issues and maximizing the health and vitality of your plants.

## ADDING YOUR MAGICKAL TOUCH

When choosing seeds for your garden, consider the magickal properties of the herbs you're growing. For example, lavender is associated with love and relaxation, while sage is often used for purification and protection. By incorporating herbs with specific magickal properties into your garden, you can enhance the energy and intention of the space.

Set up a sacred space within your garden area: Consider creating a sacred space or altar within your garden area to honor the magickal qualities of the plants you're growing. This can be a small area designated specifically for meditation, ritual, or intention-setting.

*What Is an Altar?*

An altar is a dedicated space for spiritual practice, often used for meditation, ritual, or intention-setting. It can be as simple or elaborate as you like, and should reflect your personal beliefs and spiritual path.

*Examples of Altar Decorations*

Decorate your altar with objects that speak to your senses and align with your intentions. This could include images or idols of deities or spirits you work with, crystals or gemstones, candles, flowers or herbs, tarot cards or divination tools, or other objects that hold personal significance.

When creating a magickal garden, adding images, idols, and objects that speak to your senses can greatly enhance the energy and intention of the space.

First, think about what images resonate with you. Do you have a connection to a particular deity or spiritual tradition? Adding a statue or image of that deity can serve as a focal point for your magickal workings and meditations. Alternatively, you may feel drawn to images of nature, animals, or symbols that represent your personal power. Whatever images speak to you, consider incorporating them into your garden in a way that feels meaningful.

Idols, or objects imbued with spiritual significance, can also add depth to your magickal garden. Perhaps you have a favorite crystal or a piece of jewelry that holds special meaning for you. Placing these objects in your garden can infuse the space with your personal energy and intentions. You might also consider incorporating statues or figurines that represent aspects of nature or the divine.

Consider adding objects that speak to your senses, such as wind chimes, bells, or fragrant plants. These sensory experiences can help you connect more deeply to the energy of your garden and aid in your magickal workings. Choose objects that resonate with you and that you feel drawn to, and experiment with their placement in your garden until you find a configuration that feels harmonious and powerful.

In addition to images, idols, and sensory objects, consider incorporating words of wisdom and specific colors into your magickal garden. You might choose a quote or mantra that resonates with you and place it on a stone or plaque in the garden. This serves as a reminder of your intentions and can help you stay focused during your magickal practice.

Colors also play an important role in magickal practice and can be used to enhance the energy of your garden. Different colors are associated with different energies and intentions, so consider incorporating plants, flowers, and decorative elements in colors that align with your intentions. For example, red is associated with passion and energy, while green is associated with growth and abundance. Adding pops of color throughout your garden can help to amplify the energy and create a more vibrant and magickal space.

As you add images, idols, and sensory objects to your magickal garden, be mindful of the intention you are setting for the space. Each object should be chosen with care and intention, and should contribute to the overall energy and vibe of the garden. With time and attention, your magickal garden will become a sacred space that nurtures your spiritual growth and supports your magickal practice.

## CREATING A GARDEN CALENDAR FOR THE MOON CYCLES

Are you interested in gardening and want to improve your plant's growth and productivity? Creating a garden calendar that aligns with the moon's cycle may be just what you need! By following this step-by-step guide, you'll be able to determine the best moon phase for planting each type of plant, as well as other gardening tasks such as pruning and harvesting. With a well-planned garden calendar, you can enjoy a successful and bountiful harvest all year round while aligning your garden with some witchy magick. So, let's get started!

Here's a step-by-step guide on how to make a garden calendar that aligns with the moon cycle:

1. **First, get to know the phases of the moon.** There are four main phases: new moon, waxing moon, full moon, and waning moon. Each phase has a different energy and effect on plants.

2. **Decide which plants you want to grow in your garden.** Some plants are better suited for planting during certain moon phases.

3. **Determine the best moon phase to plant each type of plant.** As a general rule, planting during the waxing moon (when the moon is increasing in size) is best for above-ground crops, while

planting during the waning moon (when the moon is decreasing in size) is best for below-ground crops.

4. **Create a calendar for the year, noting the dates of each moon phase.** You can find moon phase calendars online or in gardening books.

5. **Determine the best planting dates for each type of plant based on the moon phase calendar.** Mark these dates on your garden calendar.

6. **Consider other gardening tasks that can be aligned with the moon cycle, such as pruning, fertilizing, and harvesting.** Different moon phases are better suited for these tasks as well.

7. **Add these tasks to your garden calendar, aligning them with the appropriate moon phase.**

8. **Keep your garden calendar in a visible place so you can refer to it throughout the year.** Use it as a guide for when to plant, when to tend to your garden, and when to harvest.

By following this guide, you'll be able to create a garden calendar that aligns with the moon's phases, helping you to grow healthier and more productive plants.

Here are some guidelines on when to plant the herbs listed previously:

| Name Of Herb | Waxing | Waning |
|---|---|---|
| Peppermint | X | |
| Panax Ginseng | X | |
| Chamomile | X | |
| Mandrake Root | | X |
| Sage | X | |
| Bay Leaves | X | |
| Mugwort | X | |
| St. John's Wort | X | |
| Myrrh | | X |
| Rue | | X |
| Wormwood | | X |
| Angelica | X | |
| Hyssop | X | |
| Horsetail | | X |
| Comfrey | X | |
| Nettle | X | |
| Rosemary | X | |
| Lemon Balm | X | |
| Roses | X | |
| Geranium | X | |
| Hibiscus | X | |
| Lavender | X | |
| Lemon | X | |
| Valerian | X | |

| | | |
|---|---|---|
| Hops | X | |
| Passionflower | X | |
| Skullcap | X | |
| Eleuthero | X | |
| Schisandra | X | |
| Rhodiola Root | | X |
| Pseudostellaria Root | | X |
| Holy Basil | X | |
| Parsley | X | |
| Feverfew | X | |
| Chives | X | |
| Oregano | X | |
| Lemongrass | X | |

## CONNECT WITH THE NATURE SPIRITS

Now that you've learned how to align your garden with the moon cycle, it's time to connect with the nature spirits that inhabit your garden. These spirits can help you cultivate a healthy and thriving garden. To connect with them, spend time in your garden, preferably during a full moon. Take a deep breath and feel the energy of the plants and soil. Listen to the sounds of nature and feel the breeze on your skin. You can also offer small gifts such as herbs, flowers, or crystals to the spirits as a sign of gratitude.

There are several more ways to connect with nature spirits in your garden, and you can choose the ones that resonate with you the most. Here are some examples:

- **Meditate in your garden:** Find a quiet spot in your garden and meditate for a few minutes. This will help you connect with the energy of the plants and the Earth.
- **Create a sacred space:** Designate a specific area in your garden as a sacred space where you can connect with the spirits. Decorate it with crystals, candles, and other natural elements that resonate with you.

- **Plant with intention:** Before planting, set an intention and ask the nature spirits to guide you. This will create a deeper connection between the plants and the Earth.
- **Listen to the sounds of nature:** Sit in your garden and listen to the sounds of birds, insects, and other creatures. This will help you feel the energy of the garden and connect with the spirits that inhabit it.

Remember, connecting with the nature spirits in your garden is a personal and spiritual practice. Choose the methods that feel right for you and enjoy the magick of your garden.

By cultivating a strong relationship with the nature spirits, you can create a garden that is not only beautiful but also spiritually fulfilling. So, take some time to connect with the spirits and feel the magick of your garden.

Here are three of the most crucial steps to consider for your magickal sanctuary:

1. The first step to creating a witchy garden is to choose the right plants that align with your intentions and goals.

2. The second step is to create a garden layout that includes different areas for planting, such as a vegetable garden, herb garden, and flower garden.

3. The third step is to plant the chosen plants according to the moon cycle and to connect with the nature spirits by spending time in the garden, leaving offerings, and setting intentions.

Now that you have learned the steps to creating your witchy garden, it's time to connect with the nature spirits that inhabit it. By following the steps in this chapter, you have already started the process of building a deeper relationship with the natural world around you. In the next chapter, you will learn more about connecting with nature spirits and how this can enhance the magic of your garden. So, let's explore how you can deepen your connection to the spirits that reside in your garden.

# CHAPTER 6
# CONNECTING WITH NATURE SPIRITS

Imagine walking through a forest and coming across a majestic juniper tree. As you approach the tree, you notice that there is a small space beneath its branches that seems to be calling out to you. Curious, you step closer and feel a sense of peace wash over you. You realize that you have stumbled upon a space that has been created for nature spirits. This space has been carefully designed to invite the spirits of the forest to come and connect with the human world. In this chapter, we will explore how you can create a similar space in your garden to invite nature spirits and deepen your connection with the natural world.

## TUNING IN TO THE NATURE SPIRITS

When you talk about nature spirits, you are referring to a group of entities that are believed to exist in the natural world. These spirits are not physical beings, but rather, they are thought to be made up of etheric matter.

Nature spirits are said to be responsible for building and maintaining the plant kingdom. They are believed to work in harmony with the forces of nature to ensure that the plants grow and thrive. These spirits are thought to be the guardians of the natural world and are often associated with specific locations such as forests, rivers, and mountains.

Some people believe that nature spirits are deities that have taken on a more elemental form. They are seen as powerful forces of nature that can help or hinder humans depending on how they are approached.

In many cultures, people have developed rituals and practices to honor and communicate with nature spirits. These practices are often based on the belief that nature spirits can offer guidance, protection, and blessings to those who show them respect and reverence.

### Be Present and Grounded

As a green witch, if you want to connect with nature spirits, it's essential to be present and grounded. This means that you should focus your attention on the present moment and let go of any distractions or worries. Take some time to breathe deeply, feel your feet on the ground, and become fully aware of your surroundings.

To expand on this, you can begin by finding a quiet spot in nature, such as a forest or a park. Find a comfortable place to sit or stand and take a few deep breaths. As you breathe in, imagine that you are drawing in the energy of the Earth, and as you exhale, release any tension or negativity that you may be carrying.

Another way to connect with nature spirits is to pay attention to the signs and symbols that they may be sending you. This can include things like unusual weather patterns, unexpected encounters with animals or insects, or a sudden feeling of peace or calm. Try to be open and receptive to these messages, and see if you can interpret their meaning.

You can also establish a daily ritual or practice that helps you connect with nature. This could involve things like meditation, journaling, or simply spending time in nature each day. By making a conscious effort to connect with the natural world on a regular basis, you will begin to develop a deeper relationship with the spirits that reside there.

Finally, remember to show respect and gratitude to the nature spirits that you encounter. Offer them gifts or tokens of appreciation, and always ask for their permission before taking anything from the natural world. By showing respect and gratitude, you will create a harmonious relationship with these powerful beings and deepen your connection to the natural world.

### Be Willing and Open-Minded

To connect with nature spirits as a green witch, it's essential to have an open mind and be receptive to the idea of the existence of nature spirits. These spirits may be perceived as unseen beings that possess a strong energy that is distinct from the natural world around us.

One technique to connect with nature spirits is to imagine the Earth as a Great Spirit. This exercise can be done during meditation, in which you visualize the Earth as a living entity with its own consciousness and spirit. Try to feel a sense of respect and awe for the planet as you connect with this Great Spirit.

Another method for connecting with nature spirits is to tune into the Spirit of the Sky. Spend some time outdoors, and observe the movement of the clouds and the patterns of the wind. Try to sense the energy of the sky and feel its presence. Pay attention to any messages or insights that may come to you during this practice.

When working with nature spirits, it can be helpful to use second-person language, as if you are addressing the spirits directly. This can help to establish a stronger connection and make the experience more personal. For example, you might say, "Spirit of the Forest, I honor and respect you. Please guide me in my journey today." This can be a powerful way to connect with nature and build a deeper relationship with the natural world.

## Be Respectful and Humble

As a green witch seeking to connect with nature spirits, it's also crucial to approach these entities with a sense of respect and humility. Remember that you are entering into their world and seeking to connect with energies that are beyond human comprehension.

To establish a meaningful relationship with nature spirits, it's important to recognize that they are not there to serve you or fulfill your desires. Instead, approach them with a sense of reverence and gratitude for their presence and the role they play in the natural world.

In your interactions with nature spirits, use second-person language to acknowledge their presence and show your respect. For example, you might say, "Great Spirit of the Mountain, I come to you with deep reverence and gratitude. I honor your strength and wisdom, and I ask for your guidance as I seek to connect more deeply with the natural world."

Remember that connecting with nature spirits is not about imposing your will upon them, but rather about opening yourself up to their wisdom and energy. Approach these interactions with an open heart and a willingness to learn, and you may find that the nature spirits are more willing to reveal themselves to you in profound and transformative ways.

### Be Playful and Have Fun

Connecting with nature spirits as a Green Witch can be a joyful and playful experience. It's important to remember that nature spirits are not just serious and solemn entities, but they can also embody a sense of playfulness and lightness.

To connect with nature spirits in a fun and playful way, try spending time in nature without a specific agenda or goal in mind. Simply be present in the moment and allow yourself to explore and interact with the natural world around you.

Engage in activities that allow you to connect with the joy and wonder of nature, such as singing, dancing, or creating art inspired by the natural world. These activities can help to shift your perspective and open you up to new insights and experiences.

When interacting with nature spirits, try to approach them with a sense of playfulness and lightness. Again, use second-person language to engage with them in a fun and lighthearted way. For example, you might say, "Oh mischievous Spirit of the River, I see you hiding behind that rock! Come out and play with me!"

Remember that connecting with nature spirits is not always about serious rituals or meditation. It can also be a fun and playful experience that allows you to deepen your connection with the natural world. So go ahead and let loose, embrace your inner child, and connect with the playful energies of the nature spirits around you.

### Listen to Your Heart

It's important to listen to your heart and tune into your body. Your intuition and physical sensations can be powerful tools for connecting with the energy and wisdom of the natural world.

To connect with nature spirits in a deeper way, start by tuning into your heart and your emotions. Pay attention to the feelings that arise when you spend time in nature, and allow yourself to be open to any messages or insights that come to you.

Similarly, tune into your body and physical sensations. Pay attention to how the natural world affects you on a physical level, whether it's the feeling of the sun on your skin, the rustling of leaves in the wind, or the cool touch of water.

When interacting with nature spirits, use second-person language to address them and ask for their guidance. For example, you might say, "Spirit of the Forest, I ask that you guide me to the place where I can feel your energy most strongly. Help me to tune into my heart and my body so that I can connect with you on a deeper level."

Remember that connecting with nature spirits is not just an intellectual exercise, but also a deeply emotional experience. By listening to your heart and tuning into your body, you can deepen your connection with the natural world and access the powerful energies and wisdom of the nature spirits around you.

### Release Expectations

It's important to release any expectations or preconceptions you may have about the experience. When you approach the natural world with an open mind and heart, you allow yourself to be more receptive to the energies and messages that are present.

Try to let go of any expectations or goals you may have for the interaction to connect with nature spirits in a more authentic and meaningful way. Instead, simply be present in the moment and allow yourself to be open to whatever comes.

As above, when interacting with nature spirits, use second-person language to ask for their guidance and express your willingness to release any expectations you may have. For example, you might say, "Spirit of the Meadow, I come to you with an open heart and a willingness to release any expectations I may have. Help me to be present in this moment and to connect with your energy in the most authentic and meaningful way."

Remember that the natural world is full of surprises and unexpected gifts. By releasing your expectations and being open to the present moment, you allow yourself to experience the full richness and beauty of the natural world. Whether you receive a message from a tree, a vision from the sky, or simply a feeling of peace and connection, trust that the experience is exactly what you need in that moment.

## INVITING THE NATURE SPIRITS INTO YOUR GARDEN

To create seasonal rituals in your garden, start by observing the natural cycles and changes that occur throughout the year. Take note of the changes in the weather, the growth and bloom of plants, and the movements of animals and insects. Use this knowledge to plan rituals that celebrate and honor the energy and wisdom of the natural world.

As you plan your seasonal rituals, use second-person language to address the nature spirits and invite them into your space. For example, you might say, "Spirit of

Spring, I invite you into my garden to bring new growth and energy to this space. Help me to cultivate a thriving and abundant garden that is in harmony with the natural world."

During your seasonal rituals, incorporate elements of nature such as flowers, herbs, and stones to create a sacred and meaningful space. You might also incorporate music, dance, or meditation to deepen your connection with the energy and wisdom of the nature spirits.

Remember that your garden is a sacred space that can be a powerful source of healing and connection with the natural world. By developing seasonal rituals that honor and celebrate the energy and wisdom of the nature spirits, you can invite their presence and guidance into your space, creating a deeper sense of harmony and balance.

### Leave an Offering

Leaving an offering of food, drink, or magickal ingredients is a great way to invite nature spirits into your garden. The offerings serve as a gesture of hospitality and respect, and can also act as a source of energy and nourishment for the spirits.

When choosing what to offer, consider using natural and organic ingredients such as honey, fresh fruits, or herbs. You can also add a touch of magick to your offering by including items such as crystals, candles, or incense.

Remember to show gratitude for any gifts or signs you receive from the nature spirits, and always dispose of any offerings in a respectful and environmentally-friendly way.

### Plant Specific Flowers

Certain flowers and plants are believed to attract nature spirits, particularly fairies. To invite these spirits into your garden, consider planting flowers such as primroses, bluebells, and foxgloves. Other plants that are known to attract nature spirits include ferns, ivy, and moss.

When planting your garden, be sure to create a diverse range of habitats that can support a variety of wildlife and spirits. This can include creating shady areas for spirits that prefer cooler temperatures and incorporating structures such as birdhouses and bee hotels.

## Include Water

Water is a powerful element that can attract nature spirits and create a sense of calm and tranquility in your garden. Consider incorporating a water feature such as a small pond, fountain, or bird bath.

Be sure to keep the water clean and well-maintained to prevent the growth of algae and other harmful substances. Adding plants and stones around the water feature can also create a natural and inviting environment for nature spirits.

## Collect Small, Shiny Things

Nature spirits are often attracted to shiny and sparkly objects such as crystals, glass, and metal. Gather small shiny things and place them around your garden, either as decorative accents or hidden treasures for the spirits to discover.

When choosing your shiny objects, be mindful of their impact on the environment. Avoid using plastic or other materials that can harm wildlife and the Earth.

*Add Music*

Music can be a powerful way to connect with nature spirits and create a sense of harmony and peace in your garden. Consider playing soft and soothing music, such as nature sounds or gentle melodies, to invite the spirits into your space.

You can also create your own music by singing or playing an instrument. Remember to be mindful of the volume and timing of your music, and to respect the natural sounds of the environment and your neighbors.

*Build a Fairy House*

Building a fairy house is a fun and creative way to invite nature spirits into your garden. Use natural materials such as stones, sticks, and leaves to construct a small dwelling for the fairies and other spirits.

As you build your fairy house, be mindful of the impact on the environment and avoid damaging any living plants or creatures. Place the house in a secluded and protected area of your garden, and decorate it with natural materials such as flowers and moss.

### Be Kind to Nature

To invite nature spirits into your garden, it's important to be kind and respectful to the wildlife that shares the space with you. This can include providing food and shelter for birds and other creatures and avoiding the use of harmful chemicals and pesticides.

Create a safe and welcoming environment for wildlife by planting a diverse range of native plants, and providing water sources and nesting materials. Remember to observe and appreciate the natural beauty and diversity of the creatures that call your garden home.

### Be Good to the Earth

Finally, to invite nature spirits into your garden, it's important to be good to the Earth itself. This can include using sustainable gardening practices such as composting, mulching, and using organic fertilizers. Avoid using harsh chemicals that can harm the soil and its inhabitants, and opt for natural pest control methods. You can also consider planting native species that are well-adapted to your local ecosystem and provide food and shelter for wildlife. By treating the Earth with kindness and respect, you create a welcoming environment not just for nature spirits, but for all living beings in your garden. Additionally, by practicing sustainable gardening, you are reducing your impact on the planet and helping to protect the environment for future generations.

### Openly Welcome Them

If you want to invite nature spirits into your garden, it is important to openly welcome them. Express your desire to connect with these spirits and create a space that is inviting to them. You can do this by speaking out loud or silently in your mind, telling them that you welcome their presence in your garden.

In summary, here are three key ideas to use for connecting with nature spirits:

1. To invite nature spirits into your garden, you should openly welcome them by expressing

your desire to connect with them and create a welcoming space for them.

2. You can create physical markers in your garden, such as fairy houses or other structures made from natural materials, to show that it is a welcoming space for nature spirits.

3. Incorporating plants that are known to attract nature spirits, like daisies, marigolds, and honeysuckle, and creating a small water feature can also make your garden more inviting to these spirits. It is important to maintain a respectful attitude and avoid using harmful chemicals that could harm nature spirits and the environment.

Now that you have learned how to connect with nature spirits in your garden, you can deepen your understanding of the natural world by exploring the topic of moon cycles and gardening. Just as nature spirits are a part of the natural world, the moon also plays a significant role in the growth and development of plants. Understanding the different phases of the moon and how they affect your garden can help you to plan your planting, harvesting, and other gardening tasks more effectively. In the next chapter, you will learn about the different phases of the moon and how to use this knowledge to enhance your gardening practices.

# CHAPTER 7
# WORKING WITH THE MOON CYCLES

The moon has long been associated with magick and witchcraft. The cycles of the moon are believed to hold powerful energy that can be harnessed to manifest your intentions and desires. But did you know that the moon's power extends to gardening as well? By syncing the growth cycles of your garden with the phases of the moon, you can tap into the natural energy of the moon to enhance the health and productivity of your plants. In this chapter, you will learn more about the relationship between the moon and gardening, and how to use this knowledge to practice moon magick in your own garden.

## THE MAGICKAL POWER OF THE MOON

The moon goes through different phases or cycles as it orbits around the Earth. These phases are determined by the position of the moon in relation to the sun and the Earth. There are eight different phases of the moon, which include the new moon, waxing crescent, first quarter, waxing gibbous, full moon, waning gibbous, last quarter, and waning crescent. Each phase lasts approximately 7 days. Understanding the different phases of the moon and their corresponding energies can help you to align your intentions and goals with the natural rhythms of the universe. In the context of gardening, syncing your gardening tasks with the different phases of the moon can help to enhance the growth and vitality of your plants.

## The Moon, Witchcraft, and Spellwork

In witchcraft and spellwork, the moon's energy is believed to be unique and powerful. Each phase of the moon is associated with different types of energy and intention, and these energies can be harnessed to enhance the outcome of your spells. For example, the new moon is associated with new beginnings and fresh starts, making it a good time to cast spells related to new projects or goals. The full moon, on the other hand, is associated with abundance, manifestation, and clarity, making it a good time to cast spells related to attracting wealth or clarity of thought.

When it comes to gardening, syncing your gardening tasks with the different phases of the moon can help you to align your goals with the natural rhythms of the universe. This can be particularly helpful if you are using your garden for spellwork or intention setting. By understanding the different energies associated with each phase of the moon, you can use this knowledge to direct your intention and approach to gardening tasks in a way that is aligned with your goals and desires.

Overall, the moon's energy is believed to directly influence the outcome of spellwork and provides direction for interpreting and approaching spells. In the context of gardening, syncing your gardening tasks with the different phases of the moon can help to enhance the growth and vitality of your plants, while also providing a powerful tool for practicing moon magic in your own garden.

### The Phases of the Moon

During the New Moon phase, which marks the beginning of a new lunar cycle, the moon is invisible in the night sky. This phase is associated with new beginnings, setting intentions, and planting seeds for the future. It's a good time for starting new projects, beginning a new phase in your life, and focusing on personal growth.

As the moon begins to wax, or grow in size, during the Waxing Moon phase, the energy is ripe for manifestation, growth, and abundance. This is a great time to work on manifesting your goals, making plans, and taking action toward your desires. Use the Waxing Moon energy to bring positive change into your life.

The Full Moon is the peak of the lunar cycle and represents the culmination of energy. This phase is associated with abundance, completion, and releasing what no longer serves you. It's a great time for celebrations, rituals, and releasing negative energy. Use the Full Moon energy to amplify your intentions, charge your crystals, and release any blockages that may be holding you back.

As the moon begins to wane, or decrease in size, during the Waning Moon phase, the energy is focused on banishing, letting go, and releasing. This is a time for introspection, self-reflection, and healing. Use the Waning Moon energy to let go of negative habits, toxic relationships, and any energy that is no longer serving you.

The Dark Moon phase marks the end of the lunar cycle, just before the New Moon begins. During this phase, the moon is completely invisible in the night sky. This is a time for rest, introspection, and diving deep into the subconscious. Use the Dark Moon energy for meditation, dreamwork, and connecting with your inner self.

The moon's phases can have a significant impact on the growth of your witch garden. As the moon's gravitational pull affects the tides, it also affects the level of moisture in the soil. During the New Moon and Waxing Moon phases, the gravitational pull is weaker, which can lead to lower soil moisture. This is a good time to focus on planting above-ground crops, as they require less moisture.

During the Full Moon and Waning Moon phases, the gravitational pull is stronger. This strong gravitational pull leads to higher levels of moisture in the soil. This is a good time to focus on planting root crops, as they require more moisture. The moisture in the soil during these phases can also help seeds to germinate and take root more easily.

In addition to soil moisture, moonlight can also impact the growth of certain plants. For example, plants that produce fruits and flowers tend to do better when they receive more moonlight, while leafy greens and root crops do better with less moonlight. During the Waxing Moon and Full Moon phases, the moon provides more light, which can promote plant growth.

By paying attention to the moon's phases, you can plan and time your planting and gardening activities to maximize the growth of your witch garden. Whether you're planting herbs, flowers, or vegetables, understanding the moon's impact on soil moisture and plant growth can help you create a thriving garden.

## HOW TO HARNESS THE MOON IN YOUR GARDEN

Let's look at the different steps you should take with each stage of the moon when you're working on your magickal garden.

### New Moon

If you're looking to harness the power of the moon in your garden, the New Moon is a great time to start. During the New Moon phase, the moon is invisible in the night sky, representing a time for new beginnings and fresh starts.

One way to harness the power of the New Moon in your garden is to plant seeds. This is the perfect time to plant new seeds and set intentions for the upcoming growing season. As the moon begins to wax, or grow in size, the energy is ripe for manifestation, growth, and abundance. This energy can be harnessed to encourage your seeds to sprout and grow into healthy plants.

Here are some tips for harnessing the power of the New Moon in your garden:

1. **Clean and prepare your garden beds:** Before you plant your seeds, make sure your garden beds are clean and ready to receive them. Remove any debris, weeds, or dead plants from the area.

2. **Choose your seeds:** Select the seeds you want to plant based on your gardening goals and the plants that thrive in your climate.

3. **Set intentions:** As you plant your seeds, set intentions for the plants you are growing. Think about what you want to achieve with your garden, and visualize your plants growing healthy and strong.

4. **Water your seeds:** As you water your seeds, visualize the moon's energy nourishing them and helping them to grow.

By planting seeds during the New Moon phase and setting intentions for your garden, you can harness the power of the moon to encourage healthy growth and abundance in your garden.

### Waning Moon

The Waning Moon phase is an ideal time for letting go of things and releasing. During this phase, the moon appears to be shrinking in the night sky, and its gravitational pull is stronger. This makes it a great time to focus on the roots of your plants and help them to absorb nutrients.

Here are some tips for harnessing the power of the Waning Moon in your garden:

1. **Apply fertilizer:** The Waning Moon phase is a great time to apply fertilizer to your garden. The strong gravitational pull of the moon helps to draw the nutrients down to the roots of your plants, where they are needed the most. This can help to promote healthy growth and strong, resilient plants.

2. **Compost:** Composting is another great way to harness the power of the Waning Moon in your garden. As you compost, visualize the moon's energy breaking down the organic material and helping to nourish your plants. This nutrient-rich compost can be used to fertilize your garden and promote healthy growth.

3. **Prune:** The Waning Moon phase is also a good time to prune your plants. Removing dead or

diseased branches can help to redirect energy to the healthy parts of the plant, promoting overall growth and vitality.

By applying fertilizer, composting, and pruning during the Waning Moon phase, you can harness the power of the moon to promote healthy growth and vitality in your garden. Visualize the moon's energy nourishing your plants and helping them to thrive, and watch as your garden flourishes.

### First Quarter

The First Quarter Moon phase is a time of action and growth. During this phase, the moon appears to be half full in the night sky, and its gravitational pull is increasing. This makes it a great time to focus on planting and nourishing young plants.

Here are some tips for harnessing the power of the First Quarter Moon in your garden:

1. **Plant seedlings and young plants:** The First Quarter Moon phase is a great time to plant seedlings and young plants. The energy of the moon is focused on growth and expansion, making it an ideal time to give your plants a strong start. Choose plants that thrive in your

climate and that will provide you with a bountiful harvest.

2. **Plant leafy annual herbs:** During the First Quarter Moon phase, focus on planting leafy annual herbs like basil and parsley. These plants thrive in warm weather and require plenty of sunlight, making them a perfect fit for the energy of the First Quarter Moon. Plant them in a location that receives plenty of direct sunlight to promote healthy growth.

3. **Water and nourish your plants:** As you plant your seedlings and young plants, visualize the moon's energy nourishing them and helping them to grow strong and healthy. Water your plants regularly and use a fertilizer that is high in nitrogen to promote leaf growth.

By planting seedlings and young plants, focusing on leafy annual herbs, and nourishing your plants during the First Quarter Moon phase, you can harness the power of the moon to promote healthy growth and abundance in your garden. Visualize your plants growing tall and strong, and enjoy the fruits of your labor as they come to harvest.

## Second Quarter

The Second Quarter Moon phase is a time of growth and abundance. During this phase, the moon appears to be half full in the night sky, and its gravitational pull is increasing. This makes it a great time to focus on planting and nourishing vined annuals that yield above ground.

Here are some tips for harnessing the power of the Second Quarter Moon in your garden:

1. **Plant vined annuals:** The Second Quarter Moon phase is a great time to plant vined annuals that yield above ground. These include plants like cucumbers, beans, and peas. These plants thrive in warm weather and require plenty of sunlight, making them a perfect fit for the energy of the Second Quarter Moon. Plant them in a location that receives plenty of direct sunlight to promote healthy growth.

2. **Provide support:** As viny annuals grow, they need support to prevent them from falling over and to encourage upward growth. Install stakes or trellises before planting your vined annuals to provide support as they grow.

3. **Water and fertilize:** As you plant your vined annuals, visualize the moon's energy nourishing

them and helping them to grow strong and healthy. Water your plants regularly and use a fertilizer that is high in phosphorus to promote flowering and fruiting.

By planting vined annuals, providing support, and nourishing your plants during the Second Quarter Moon phase, you can harness the power of the moon to promote healthy growth and abundance in your garden. Visualize your plants climbing tall and strong, and enjoy the fruits of your labor as they come to harvest.

### Full Moon

The Full Moon phase is a time of peak energy and abundance. During this phase, the moon is fully illuminated in the night sky, and its gravitational pull is at its strongest. This makes it a great time to focus on weeding your garden and planting root vegetables and flower bulbs.

Here are some tips for effectively capturing the power of the Full Moon in your garden:

1. **Weed your garden:** The Full Moon phase is a great time to weed your garden. The increased gravitational pull of the moon during this phase

makes it easier to pull out weeds and other unwanted plants. Take advantage of this energy to clear out any weeds that may be competing with your plants for nutrients and sunlight.

2. **Plant root vegetables:** During the Full Moon phase, focus on planting root vegetables like carrots, beets, and potatoes. These plants thrive when planted during the Full Moon, as the increased gravitational pull of the moon helps to promote healthy root growth. Plant them in a location that receives plenty of sunlight to promote healthy growth.

3. **Plant flower bulbs:** The Full Moon phase is also a great time to plant flower bulbs like tulips, daffodils, and hyacinths. These plants require a period of cold weather to trigger their growth, and planting them during the Full Moon can help to promote healthy growth and vibrant blooms come springtime.

By weeding your garden, planting root vegetables, and planting flower bulbs during the Full Moon phase, you can harness the power of the moon to promote healthy growth and abundance in your garden. Visualize your plants growing deep, strong roots and producing beautiful flowers and bountiful harvests.

### Third Quarter/Waning Moon

The Third Quarter/Waning Moon phase is a time of reflection and preparation. During this phase, the moon appears to be half full in the night sky, and its gravitational pull is decreasing. This makes it a great time to focus on transplanting, pruning, harvesting, and fertilizing your garden. Additionally, it is a great time to plant biennials, perennials, bulbs, and root herbs.

Here are some tips for harnessing the power of the Third Quarter/Waning Moon in your garden:

1. **Transplanting:** The Third Quarter/Waning Moon phase is a great time to transplant any plants that may need to be moved to a different location in your garden. The decreased gravitational pull of the moon during this phase makes it easier to transplant your plants without causing too much stress to the roots. Make sure to water your plants thoroughly after transplanting to help them settle into their new location.

2. **Pruning:** During the Third Quarter/Waning Moon phase, focus on pruning any dead or diseased branches from your trees and shrubs. This will help to promote healthy growth and

prevent the spread of disease throughout your garden.

3. **Harvesting:** The Third Quarter/Waning Moon phase is also a great time to harvest any fruits, vegetables, or herbs that may be ready. This is the time when the energy of the plant is focused on the roots, making it a good time to harvest root vegetables like carrots, beets, and potatoes.

4. **Fertilizing:** During the Third Quarter/Waning Moon phase, focus on fertilizing your garden with a balanced fertilizer. This will help to promote healthy growth and prepare your plants for the next phase of growth.

5. **Plant biennials, perennials, bulbs, and root herbs:** The Third Quarter/Waning Moon phase is a great time to plant biennials, perennials, bulbs, and root herbs. These plants require a strong root system to survive and thrive, making the Third Quarter/Waning Moon phase the perfect time to plant them. Make sure to plant them in a location that receives plenty of sunlight and water them regularly to promote healthy growth.

By transplanting, pruning, harvesting, fertilizing, and planting biennials, perennials, bulbs, and root herbs during the Third Quarter/Waning Moon phase, you can harness the power of the moon to promote healthy growth and abundance in your garden. Visualize your plants growing strong, healthy roots and producing bountiful harvests.

### Last Quarter

During the Last Quarter phase, the moon appears to be half full in the sky, and its gravitational pull is decreasing. This makes it a great time to focus on improving your soil and taking care of any pests that may be lurking in your garden.

Here are some tips for harnessing the power of the Last Quarter in your garden:

1. **Focus on improving soil:** During the Last Quarter phase, focus on improving your soil quality by adding compost, manure, or other organic matter. This will help to replenish nutrients in the soil and promote healthy growth for your plants. Use a garden fork or tiller to work the compost into the soil, making sure to avoid damaging any roots.
2. **Take care of pests:** During the Last Quarter phase, it is a good time to take care of any pests that may be causing problems in your garden. Use organic methods such as handpicking,

spraying with insecticidal soap or neem oil, or introducing beneficial insects to help control the pest population. This will help to prevent further damage to your plants and promote healthy growth.

By focusing on improving your soil quality and taking care of pests during the Last Quarter phase, you can harness the power of the moon to promote healthy growth and abundance in your garden. Take the time to reflect on the progress you have made so far, and visualize the healthy and vibrant garden you will have in the future.

Good Rules to Follow

A good rule of thumb to follow when harnessing the power of the moon for your garden is to plant flowers and plants that bear crops above ground during the Waxing Moon phase, and plant flowers and plants with crops below ground during the Waning Moon phase.

During the Waxing Moon phase, the moon appears to be growing in the sky, and its gravitational pull is increasing. This makes it a great time to plant and promote growth for flowers and plants that bear crops above ground such as tomatoes, beans, peas, and herbs like basil and parsley.

On the other hand, during the Waning Moon phase, the moon appears to be decreasing in the sky, and its gravitational pull is decreasing. This makes it a great time to focus on planting and promoting growth for flowers and plants with crops below ground such as potatoes, onions, carrots, and bulbs like tulips and daffodils.

By following these rules, you can work in harmony with the natural phases of the moon to promote healthy growth and abundance in your garden. Take the time to reflect on your goals and intentions for your garden, and visualize the healthy and vibrant garden you will have in the future. Enjoy the beauty and abundance that comes with working with the cycles of the moon.

Here are the three most vital points to consider when incorporating the moon into your garden work:

1. Understanding the different phases of the moon can be helpful in planning and achieving your goals. By aligning your actions with the moon cycles, you can take advantage of the energy and influence of each phase.
2. The New Moon is a time for setting intentions and starting new projects, while the Full Moon is a time for releasing what no longer serves you and celebrating your accomplishments. The Waxing Moon is a time for growth and

expansion, while the Waning Moon is a time for reflection and introspection.

3. You can work with the moon cycles by tracking the phases of the moon and planning your activities accordingly. You can also incorporate moon rituals, such as meditation or journaling, to help you connect with the energy of each phase and manifest your goals.

By understanding the moon cycles and how they can affect the growth of plants, you can optimize your harvest of herbs and other crops. The phase of the moon can influence the quality and potency of herbs, so it's important to harvest them at the right time. In the next chapter on harvesting herbs, you will learn about the different moon phases and how they relate to the harvesting of herbs. You will also discover tips for harvesting herbs, such as harvesting during the right phase of the moon and using proper techniques to ensure the best possible yield. With this knowledge, you can cultivate a bountiful and thriving herb garden that is aligned with the natural rhythms of the moon.

# CHAPTER 8

# How to Harvest Your Magickal Herbs

A s the wise Gertrude Jekyll once said, "The love of gardening is a seed once sown that never dies" (Catherine, 2020). In this chapter, you will learn about the different ways of using herbs as a green witch, harvesting, spellwork, and rituals. However, harvesting is not just about picking the plants at random. It requires just as much care as planting the seeds, as the quality and potency of the herbs can depend on the timing and technique of the harvest. By understanding the best practices for harvesting, you can ensure that your herbs are of the highest quality and are ready for use in your magickal workings. So, get ready to delve into the world of herb harvesting and discover the secrets to unlocking the full potential of your garden.

## KNOWING THE RIGHT TIME TO PICK YOUR HERBS

Knowing the right time to pick your herbs is crucial for ensuring their quality and potency. Let's look at the importance of choosing the correct time of year and the perfect time of day when you harvest your herbs for spellwork.

### *Time of Year (Season)*

As a green witch, timing is everything when it comes to harvesting herbs, and the season in which you harvest can significantly impact their quality and potency. For most leafy herbs, such as basil and parsley, the best time to harvest is usually in mid-spring to summer when they are in full bloom. This is when they have the highest concentration of essential oils, making them more flavorful and aromatic.

It's important to pay attention to the changes in your herbs as the seasons progress. As summer transitions to fall, some herbs may begin to lose their essential oils and flavors, making them less potent. In contrast, other herbs, such as rosemary, tend to grow more robustly in cooler weather and may be best harvested in late fall or early winter.

By understanding the seasonal changes in your herbs, you can plan your harvests accordingly and ensure that you're picking them at their peak flavor and potency. This knowledge can also help you to better plan for the long-term storage of your herbs, as different seasons may require different preservation methods.

In addition to the season, it's also important to consider the moon's cycle when harvesting your herbs. Some green witches believe that the moon's energy can influence the quality and potency of herbs, and they may choose to harvest their herbs during specific phases of the moon for different purposes. By incorporating both seasonal and lunar timing into your herb harvesting practices, you can create a deeper connection with the natural rhythms of the Earth and harness the full power of your herbs.

### Time of Day

When it comes to figuring out when to pick herbs, it's important to pay attention to the time of day. To get the most flavor and potency from your herbs, it's recommended that you pick leaves in the early morning before the sun is at its strongest. The essential oils are at their highest concentration during this period.

For flowers, the best time to pick them is in the late morning when the dew has dried off, but before the sun gets too hot. This is because the essential oils in the flowers are still strong, but the heat of the day hasn't caused them to evaporate yet.

When it comes to fruits, berries, and seeds, it's best to wait until the late afternoon to pick them. This is because they need time to fully ripen and develop their flavors throughout the day. By the late afternoon, they should be at their peak flavor and nutrition.

It's important to keep in mind that these guidelines may vary depending on the specific type of herb you're growing, as well as the climate and growing conditions in your area. So, be sure to do your research and consult with experienced herb growers in your area to get the best results. By following these tips, you can ensure that you're harvesting your herbs at the optimal time to get the most out of your harvest.

## HARVESTING YOUR HERBS

Before you harvest your herbs there are a lot of different things you must consider if you want to do it properly. Correctly harvested herbs with the optimum intentions behind them are by far the most effective to use in spellwork.

### Use the Right Tools

If you're planning on harvesting your herbs, there are a few tips you should keep in mind to ensure that you do it properly. First and foremost, it's important to use the right tools for the job. For non-woody herbs like basil or cilantro, you can simply use your fingertips to pinch off the leaves or stems. However, for more woody or fibrous herbs like rosemary or thyme, it's best to use a pair of snips or pruners to make clean cuts that won't damage the plant.

When harvesting your herbs, be sure to only take what you need and leave enough behind so that the plant can continue to grow and produce more leaves or flowers. It's also important to harvest your herbs regularly, as this can help to promote new growth and keep the plant healthy. Harvest with only the purest intentions and be sure to thank the plant as you work. You can do this by saying a little thank you out loud or just by setting your intentions as you harvest.

Another important tip is to harvest your herbs when they are at their peak flavor and potency. This can vary depending on the type of herb you're growing, but generally, you should aim to harvest your herbs in the morning after the dew has dried, but before the sun gets too hot. This is when the essential oils in the leaves or flowers are at their highest concentration.

### Harvesting for Growth

If you want to properly harvest your herbs and encourage healthy growth, there are a few tips you should keep in mind. Firstly, make sure that you're harvesting your herbs for growth. This means that you should avoid harvesting too much at once, especially when the plant is still young. Instead, take only a few leaves or stems from each plant at a time, and allow the plant to recover before harvesting more.

For herbs that have a branching growth habit, like basil or mint, it's best to harvest from the top of each stem, just above where two new branches are emerging. This will encourage the plant to produce new branches and leaves, leading to a fuller, bushier plant.

Regular trimming is also essential for promoting new growth in your herbs. By trimming off the top few inches of each stem on a regular basis, you can encourage the plant to grow more vigorously and produce more leaves and flowers.

Finally, when harvesting herbs like cilantro or parsley, look for plants with leaves or stalks emerging from the soil right at the base. These herbs are best harvested by taking the entire plant, roots and all, rather than just the leaves or stems. This will ensure that you get the freshest, most flavorful herbs possible.

### Harvesting Herbs for Flowers

If you're growing herbs for their flowers, there are a few tips you should keep in mind when it comes time to harvest them. Firstly, make sure that you're harvesting your herbs at the right time. Different herbs will bloom at different times, so it's important to research the specific timing for each herb in your garden.

When harvesting herbs for their flowers, it's best to wait until the flowers are fully open before harvesting. This is when the flowers will be at their most fragrant and flavorful. Use sharp scissors or pruning shears to cut the stem just below the flower head, being careful not to damage the surrounding foliage.

If you're planning to use the flowers for culinary purposes, be sure to rinse them gently in cool water and allow them to dry completely before using. You can also dry the flowers by hanging them upside down in a dark, well-ventilated area.

Keep in mind that harvesting herbs for their flowers can be an on-going process. As long as you continue to deadhead the spent flowers, new flowers will continue to emerge, providing you with a steady supply of fragrant and flavorful blooms throughout the growing season.

### *Harvesting Herbs for Seeds*

If you're growing herbs for their seeds, there are a few tips you should keep in mind when it comes time to harvest them. Firstly, make sure that you're harvesting your herbs at the right time. Different herbs will produce seeds at different times, so it's important to research the specific timing for each herb in your garden.

When harvesting herbs for their seeds, it's best to wait until the seed heads have fully matured and turned brown or black. This is a sign that the seeds are fully formed and ready to be harvested. Use sharp scissors or pruning shears to cut the stem just below the seed head, being careful not to damage the surrounding foliage.

Once you've harvested the seed heads, place them in a paper bag or envelope and allow them to dry completely in a warm, dry, and well-ventilated area. Once the seeds are fully dry, you can remove them from the seed heads by rubbing them gently between your fingers.

If you're planning to save the seeds for future planting, be sure to store them in a cool, dark, and dry place in an airtight container. This will help to ensure that the seeds remain viable and ready to plant when the next growing season arrives.

### Considering the Moon Phase

You should aim to harvest your herbs during the last phase of the waning moon. This is because during this time, the moon's gravitational pull is decreasing, which is said to make the sap flow in the opposite direction, towards the roots of the plant. This can help to improve the flavor and aroma of the herbs.

To harvest your herbs during the last phase of the waning moon, it's important to keep track of the lunar cycle. You can use a lunar calendar or digital app to help you with this. Once you've identified the right time, use the tips mentioned earlier to harvest your herbs using the right tools and techniques.

## DRYING AND STORING HERBS

If you're growing your own herbs, one of the benefits is having a fresh supply on hand whenever you need it. However, there may be times when you have more herbs than you can use fresh. In these cases, drying and storing your herbs is a great way to preserve them for later use. Properly dried and stored herbs can retain their flavor and aroma for months, allowing you to enjoy the taste and benefits of your garden long after the growing season has ended. In this section, we'll provide you with some tips on how to dry and store your herbs effectively.

### Drying Herbs

If you're looking to dry your herbs for later use, there are a few methods you can try. One popular method is air-drying your herbs by hanging them upside down. To do this, gather a small bunch of herbs together and tie them with a string. Choose a warm, well-ventilated and dry area where you will hang the bundles upside down. The herbs will dry out over time, and you can remove the leaves from the stems once they are completely dry.

If you prefer a faster method, you can also dry your herbs in the oven. Preheat your oven to its lowest temperature setting and then, spread the herbs out in a thin layer on a baking sheet. Place the baking sheet in the oven and leave the door slightly ajar to allow moisture to escape. Check the herbs frequently and remove them from the oven once they are dry and crumbly.

Regardless of the method you choose, it's important to make sure that your herbs are completely dry before storing them. Any remaining moisture can cause your herbs to mold or spoil over time.

When storing your dried herbs, choose airtight containers that will keep out moisture and light. Glass jars with tight-fitting lids are a popular choice. Label your containers with the name of the herb and the date it was dried to help you keep track of freshness. To retain the taste and scent of your herbs for an extended period, store them in a cool, dry, and dimly lit location.

### Freezing Herbs

Another great way to preserve your herbs is by freezing them. Freezing can help retain the fresh flavor and aroma of your herbs for longer periods of time.

To freeze your herbs, you can start by washing and cutting them into small pieces and packing them into ice cube trays. Fill each compartment with the chopped herbs and then add water or olive oil to cover them. Once frozen, remove the cubes and store them in a labeled plastic bag in the freezer. You can easily drop these herb cubes into soups, stews, and other dishes throughout the year.

Alternatively, you can freeze individual leaves by spreading them out on a cookie sheet and placing them in the freezer. Once frozen, transfer the leaves to a labeled plastic bag for long-term storage.

If you have larger herb sprigs, you can wrap them tightly in plastic wrap or aluminum foil and place them in an airtight freezer container. Make sure to label the container with the name and date of the herbs.

When you're ready to use your frozen herbs, simply thaw them out in the refrigerator or add them directly to your dish while they're still frozen. Freezing herbs is a great way to have a fresh supply of your favorite herbs on hand year-round.

### Storing Herbs

Properly storing your herbs is crucial to maintaining their flavor and potency. You'll want to keep them in a cool, dark area and away from direct sunlight. Light can cause the herbs to lose their flavor and color, so it's helpful to store them in colored glass jars or ceramic containers that block out light.

Make sure the container you choose is airtight to prevent moisture from getting in and damaging the herbs. Labeling the container with the name of the herb and the date it was stored will help you keep track of its freshness.

If you have a large collection of herbs, consider organizing them alphabetically or by category in a storage box or cabinet. This will help you easily locate the herb you need when preparing a recipe.

Storing your herbs properly can help extend their shelf life and preserve their flavor for longer periods of time. With a little care and attention, you can enjoy the benefits of fresh herbs all year round.

Let's go over three of the most important aspects of harvesting our precious herbs:

1. When harvesting herbs, it's important to use the right tools for the job, such as snips or pruners for precise cuts that won't damage the plant.

2. You can preserve your herbs by hanging them to air-dry, drying them in the oven at a low temperature, freezing them in ice cube trays, spreading them out on a cookie sheet, or wrapping them tightly and storing them in an air-tight container.

3. To store your herbs properly, you'll want to keep them out of direct sunlight, store them in airtight containers that block out light, and label the containers with the name of the herb and the date it was stored. Storing your herbs correctly will help extend their shelf life and preserve their flavor.

Now that you know how to properly harvest and preserve your herbs, it's time to put them to good use by exploring some delicious and nutritious herbal recipes. In the next chapter, we'll dive into a variety of recipes that showcase the unique flavors and health benefits of herbs. From savory soups and stews to refreshing teas and tonics, you'll discover new and exciting ways to incorporate herbs into your daily diet. So, let's get cooking and start exploring the wonderful world of herbal recipes!

# CHAPTER 9

# RECIPES FOR REMEDIES AND CURES

D id you know that many of the medicinal compounds we use today can be traced back to the plant-based remedies used by witches in centuries past? "Witches' brews" played a key role in the development of modern medicine. From powerful painkillers to potent antibiotics, many of today's most important drugs have their roots in the herbal concoctions brewed by healers and witches alike (Thompson, 2014). In this chapter, we'll explore some of the healing preparations you can make using various witchy plants, from teas to incense. Whether you're looking to boost your immunity, ease your anxiety, or soothe a sore throat, these herbal remedies can help you harness the power of nature to promote health and well-being. So, let's start exploring the fascinating world of witchy plant-based medicine!

## EXPLORING MAGICKAL REMEDIES

Herbal remedies have been used for centuries to promote health and well-being, and to treat a wide range of ailments and conditions. From teas and tinctures to oils and salves, there are countless ways to use plants and herbs to support your body and mind. Whether you're looking to ease anxiety, boost your immunity, or soothe a sore throat, there's likely an herbal remedy that can help. Some herbal remedies are used to address specific physical symptoms, such as headaches or digestive issues, while others are believed to promote spiritual or emotional healing, such as aromatherapy or herbal baths. In this chapter, we'll explore some of the most popular and effective herbal remedies used by witches and healers, and we'll look at the science behind how they work. So, whether you're a seasoned practitioner or just starting to explore the world of magickal remedies, there's something here for you!

### Different Types of Herbal Remedies

Herbal remedies come in various forms and can be used in different ways to treat different ailments.

One of the most common ways to consume herbs is through tea. Herbal tea is an infusion made by steeping herbs in boiling water. Different herbs can be blended together to create a unique flavor and therapeutic effect.

One way to use herbs topically is by making salves and ointments. To make them, you will need to infuse herbs into oil and then add beeswax to create a solid consistency. Here's how to do it:

**Ingredients:**

- 1 cup of carrier oil (such as olive oil, coconut oil, or almond oil)
- ¼ cup of dried herbs
- ¼ cup of beeswax pellets

**Instructions:**

1. Heat the carrier oil and herbs in a double boiler or a heat-safe glass bowl set over a pot of simmering water.
2. Let the herbs infuse in the oil for 1 to 2 hours, stirring occasionally.
3. After the oil is infused, strain it through a cheesecloth or fine-mesh strainer into a clean bowl.
4. Return the infused oil to the double boiler or glass bowl and add the beeswax pellets.
5. Heat the mixture until the beeswax has melted, stirring occasionally.
6. Once the beeswax is melted, pour the mixture into clean jars or tins.
7. Let the mixture cool and solidify before using.
8. Apply the salve or ointment directly to the affected area as needed.

Adding herbs to bath water is a soothing way to use herbal remedies. A handful of dried herbs can be added to a warm bath to create a relaxing and healing experience.

Tinctures can be a way of using herbs for medicinal and magickal purposes. A tincture is a concentrated liquid extract made by soaking herbs in alcohol or vinegar. Tinctures can be taken orally or added to teas for a potent effect.

Herbal shrubs are a fantastic way to enjoy the magickal benefits of herbs. These are a type of vinegar-based drink made with fresh herbs, vinegar, and sweetener. Shrubs can be used to aid digestion, boost the immune system, and provide a refreshing drink.

Finally, infused oils are an easy and popular way to use herbs. These are made by soaking herbs in oil for several weeks to infuse the oil with the plant's properties. Infused oils can be used in cooking or applied topically for their therapeutic effects.

Knowing the different types of herbal remedies and their benefits can help you choose the right method for your specific needs.

## Guidelines for Taking Remedies

When taking herbal remedies, it's important to keep in mind that they are not the same as pharmaceutical medicine. You should watch for any potential side effects and be aware of any allergic reactions you may have to certain herbs. It's also a good idea to consult with a professional, such as a naturopathic doctor or herbalist, to ensure that you are taking the right herbs for your particular needs and that they won't interact with any medications you may be taking. By taking these precautions, you can safely and effectively use herbal remedies to promote your health and well-being.

## TEA AND LONG INFUSION RECIPES

Here are some examples of tea or long infusion recipes that you can make using the herbs from your magickal garden:

### *Lemon Balm Tea*

Lemon balm tea is a soothing and refreshing remedy that can help with stress, anxiety, and sleeplessness. This recipe uses dried lemon balm leaves, which can be easily obtained from health food stores or online herbal shops.

## Ingredients:

- 2 tablespoons of dried lemon balm leaves
- 2 cups of water
- Honey or lemon (optional)

## Instructions:

1. Bring water to a boil in a small pot or tea kettle.
2. Add dried lemon balm leaves to a tea infuser or a tea bag.
3. Pour boiling water over the tea infuser or tea bag, covering it completely.
4. Cover and let the tea steep for about 5–10 minutes.
5. Remove the infuser or tea bag and discard the leaves.
6. Add honey or lemon to taste, if desired.
7. Serve and enjoy!

### *Pregnancy Tea*

This herbal tea is formulated to support the health and well-being of pregnant women. The combination of herbs helps to strengthen the uterus, nourish the body, and support a healthy pregnancy.

**Ingredients:**

- 1 cup red raspberry leaf
- 1 cup nettle leaf
- 1 cup alfalfa leaf
- ½ cup oatstraw
- Honey (optional)

**Instructions:**

1. Combine 1 cup of red raspberry leaf, 1 cup of nettle leaf, 1 cup of alfalfa leaf, and ½ cup of oatstraw in a large bowl or jar.
2. Mix well and store in an airtight container.
3. To make the tea, bring 1 quart (4 cups) of water to a boil and remove from heat.
4. Add ¼ cup of the herb mixture to the water and stir.
5. Cover and let steep for at least 30 minutes, or up to 4 hours.
6. Strain the tea and sweeten with honey, if desired.
7. Drink 1–3 cups per day, starting in the second trimester.

Note: It's always a good idea to check with your healthcare provider before consuming any herbal remedies during pregnancy.

### Mint and Lavender Tea

This herbal tea is formulated to provide a soothing and relaxing effect. Mint is known for its calming properties, while lavender has a relaxing effect that helps to reduce stress and anxiety.

**Ingredients:**

- 1–2 teaspoons dried mint leaves
- 1–2 teaspoons dried lavender flowers
- 2 cups water

**Instructions:**

1. Boil 2 cups of water in a pot or kettle.
2. Add 1–2 teaspoons of dried mint leaves and 1–2 teaspoons of dried lavender flowers to a tea infuser or tea bag.
3. Place the infuser or tea bag in a teapot or mug.
4. Pour the hot water over the infuser or tea bag.
5. Cover and let steep for 5–10 minutes.
6. Remove the infuser or tea bag and discard.
7. Enjoy your mint and lavender tea.

Note: You can adjust the amount of herbs and steeping time to your preference. You can also add honey or lemon for taste.

### Nettle Infusion

This herbal infusion is formulated to provide a nutrient-rich drink that can help with a variety of health concerns. Nettle leaves are rich in vitamins and minerals, including iron, calcium, and vitamin C, and are believed to support the immune system, reduce inflammation, and promote healthy digestion.

**Ingredients:**

- 1 oz dried nettle leaves
- 1 quart water

**Instructions:**

1. Boil 1 quart of water in a pot or kettle.
2. Measure out 1 oz of dried nettle leaves.
3. Add the nettle leaves to a quart-sized mason jar.
4. Pour the boiling water over the nettle leaves, filling the jar to the top.
5. Cover the jar with a lid and let steep for at least 4 hours, or overnight.

6. Strain the nettle infusion into a pitcher or another jar.
7. Drink the infusion throughout the day, either hot or cold.

Note: You can add honey, lemon, or other herbs to the nettle infusion to enhance the flavor. It's important to drink plenty of water along with the nettle infusion, as it has a diuretic effect. It's also a good idea to start with a small amount and gradually increase the amount of nettle used, as it can cause an allergic reaction in some people.

### Stress Relief Tea—Hot Infusion

The purpose of this remedy is to promote relaxation, reduce feelings of anxiety and tension, and help soothe the mind and body.

The herbs used in this tea typically include chamomile, lemon balm, and lavender. Chamomile is known for its calming properties, while lemon balm can help reduce anxiety and promote relaxation. Lavender is also known for its calming effects and can help relieve tension.

## Ingredients:

- 1 tablespoon dried chamomile flowers
- 1 tablespoon dried lemon balm leaves
- 1 teaspoon dried lavender flowers
- 2 cups water

## Instructions:

1. Boil 2 cups of water in a tea kettle or on the stove.
2. While the water is boiling, place 1 tablespoon of dried chamomile flowers, 1 tablespoon of dried lemon balm leaves, and 1 teaspoon of dried lavender flowers into a tea infuser or a teapot.
3. Once the water has boiled, pour it over the herbs in the tea infuser or teapot.
4. Cover the tea infuser or teapot and allow the tea to steep for 5–10 minutes.
5. After the tea has steeped, remove the tea infuser or strain the tea through a fine mesh strainer into a cup.
6. Enjoy the tea hot, adding sweetener or milk if desired.

## Moon Tea—Cold Infusion by the Light of the Moon

Moon Tea is a cold-infused herbal tea that is made by steeping herbs in water overnight under the light of the moon. This unique method of preparation is believed to enhance the energy and potency of the herbs.

This remedy is known to harness the energy of the moon and the healing properties of herbs to create a powerful, calming tea that promotes relaxation and overall well-being.

The herbs used in this tea can vary depending on your desired effect. Some common herbs used in Moon Tea include chamomile, lavender, lemon balm, and rose petals. Chamomile and lavender are known for their calming properties, while lemon balm can help reduce anxiety and promote relaxation. Rose petals can help promote feelings of love and well-being.

**Other ingredients:**

- 4 cups of water

**Instructions:**

1. Select your herbs and chop them into small pieces.
2. Take a clean glass jar and add ¼ cup of the chosen herbs.
3. Fill the jar with 4 cups of water, leaving about an inch of space at the top.
4. Place the jar outside under the light of the moon (preferably a full moon) but away from direct sunlight. Let the herbs steep in the water for at least 8 hours, or overnight.
5. In the morning, strain the tea through a fine mesh strainer into a clean glass jar or pitcher.
6. Chill the tea in the refrigerator and enjoy it cold, adding sweetener or lemon if desired.

### *Four Thieves Vinegar*

The purpose of Four Thieves Vinegar is to protect against illness and promote overall health. The herbal combination is believed to have antibacterial, antiviral, and antifungal properties, which can help protect the body from a range of infectious diseases.

## Ingredients:

- 4 cloves garlic, chopped
- 2 tablespoons fresh rosemary, chopped
- 2 tablespoons fresh sage, chopped
- 2 tablespoons fresh thyme, chopped
- 2 tablespoons fresh lavender, chopped
- 2 tablespoons fresh peppermint, chopped
- 2 cups apple cider vinegar

## Instructions:

1. Gather the herbs and chop them into small pieces.
2. Combine the chopped herbs with 2 cups of apple cider vinegar in a glass jar.
3. Cover the jar with a non-reactive lid (such as a plastic lid or wax paper) to prevent the vinegar from corroding the lid.
4. Store the jar in a cool, dark place for 4 to 6 weeks, shaking the jar every day to ensure the herbs are well-distributed.
5. After 4 to 6 weeks, strain the vinegar through cheesecloth or a fine mesh strainer into a clean jar.

6. The Four Thieves Vinegar is now ready to use. It can be added to salads or used as a marinade, taken as a tonic, or used as a cleaning agent.

Note: You can add things like honey or a little sugar if you prefer a sweeter remedy.

### Herb-Infused Oils for Wellness and Beauty

Herb-infused oils are a great way to incorporate the healing properties of herbs into your wellness and beauty routine. These oils can be used as massage oils, added to lotions or salves, used as hair treatments, or even added to your bath.

Choose an herb that aligns with the purpose of your oil. For example, if you are making a relaxation oil, you might choose lavender or chamomile. For a skin-soothing oil, calendula or comfrey could be used.

The purpose of the remedy will depend on the herb you choose. Herb-infused oils can be used for a variety of purposes, such as relaxation, skin-soothing, pain relief, or hair treatment.

**Ingredients:**

- 1 cup fresh or dried herbs
- 2 cups carrier oil (such as olive oil, sweet almond oil, or jojoba oil)
- 1 teaspoon vitamin E oil (optional, for preservation)

**Instructions:**

1. Start by harvesting or purchasing fresh or dried herbs. If using fresh herbs, make sure to wash and dry them thoroughly before using.
2. Fill a 16 oz glass jar with your chosen herb, packing it in tightly.
3. Cover the herbs with 2 cups of your chosen carrier oil, making sure the herbs are completely submerged.

4. Add 1 teaspoon of vitamin E oil to the jar (if desired) to help preserve the oil.

5. Cover the jar with a tight-fitting lid and store it in a warm, dark place for 4 to 6 weeks. Shake the jar daily to ensure the herbs are well-distributed throughout the oil.

6. After 4 to 6 weeks, strain the oil through a cheesecloth or fine-mesh strainer into a clean jar or bottle.

7. Label your oil with the herb used and the date it was made, and store it in a cool, dark place.

Using herb-infused oils is easy. Simply apply the oil to your skin, hair, or scalp and massage gently. You can also add a few drops of essential oil to your herb-infused oil for added benefits and fragrance.

## HAND-POURED HERBAL CANDLES

Hand-poured herbal candles are a delightful way to incorporate herbs into your daily self-care routine.

The purpose of these candles is to promote relaxation, calm, and well-being through the use of aromatherapy and herbal medicine.

The herbs used in these candles can vary depending on the desired effect. Some common herbs used in herbal candles include lavender, chamomile, peppermint, and rosemary. Lavender is known for its calming properties, while chamomile can help reduce anxiety and promote relaxation. Peppermint is invigorating and can help with focus and mental clarity. Rosemary is stimulating and can help promote a sense of energy and vitality.

**Ingredients:**

- 1 pound of soy wax flakes
- Candle wicks
- Essential oils (optional)
- Candle dye (optional)

**Instructions:**

1. Melt 1 pound of soy wax flakes in a double boiler or a heat-safe glass bowl set over a pot of boiling water.
2. While the wax is melting, prepare your candle containers by placing the wicks in the center and securing them with a drop of melted wax. You can use any kind of container that resonates with you including repurposing old mason jars or candle jars.
3. Once the wax is melted, remove it from the heat and allow it to cool slightly.
4. Stir in 1–2 tablespoons of dried herbs, 10–20 drops of essential oils (if using), and a few drops of candle dye (if using).
5. Pour the melted wax into your prepared candle containers, filling them about ¾ of the way full.

6. Allow the candles to cool and harden completely before trimming the wicks to ¼ inch and using them.

## HERBAL TINCTURES

Herbal tinctures are a popular method of using herbs for their medicinal properties. The purpose of a tincture is to extract the medicinal properties of an herb in a concentrated form that is easy to take. Tinctures are often used to support the immune system, aid in digestion, promote relaxation and support overall health and well-being.

The herb used in tinctures can vary depending on the desired effect. Some common herbs used in tinctures include echinacea, ginger, chamomile, and milk thistle. Echinacea is known for its immune-boosting properties, while ginger can help with digestion and nausea. Chamomile is relaxing and can help with anxiety and sleep, while milk thistle is supportive of liver function.

**Ingredients:**

- Herb of your choice
- High-proof alcohol (such as vodka or brandy)
- Distilled water (optional)

**Instructions:**

1. Fill a glass jar 1/3 to 1/2 full with the herb.
2. Cover the herb completely with high-proof alcohol, leaving 1 inch of headspace at the top.
3. Stir the mixture to ensure the herb is completely submerged.

4. Seal the jar tightly and store it in a cool, dark place for 4 to 6 weeks, shaking daily to mix well.

5. After 4 to 6 weeks, strain the mixture through a cheesecloth or fine-mesh strainer into a clean jar.

6. Press down on the herbs to extract as much liquid as possible.

7. If desired, add distilled water to dilute the tincture to the desired strength.

8. Label the jar with the name of the herb and the date it was made.

Overall, tinctures are a convenient and effective way to use herbs for their medicinal properties. They are easy to take and can be customized to your specific needs and preferences. With regular use, tinctures can help support overall health and well-being and provide targeted support for specific health concerns. However, it's important to consult with a healthcare professional before using any herbal remedies, especially if you have a medical condition or are taking medication.

## INCENSE RECIPES

Incense is a popular tool used in magick and rituals for its ability to enhance and direct energy. Following are some recipes for different types of incense:

### Protection Incense

**Herbs used:** Sage, bay leaves, rosemary, and cinnamon.

**Other ingredients:** Frankincense resin, charcoal.

**Purpose of the remedy:** This incense is designed to provide spiritual protection and ward off negative energy.

**Instructions:**

1. Grind the herbs and frankincense resin into a fine powder using a mortar and pestle.
2. Add a small amount of the mixture to a charcoal disc, and allow it to smolder and release its fragrance.

## Cleansing Incense

**Herbs used:** Cedar, lavender, and white sage.

**Other ingredients:** Frankincense resin, charcoal.

**Purpose of the remedy:** This incense is designed to cleanse and purify a space or person.

**Instructions:**

1. Grind the herbs and frankincense resin into a fine powder using a mortar and pestle.
2. Add a small amount of the mixture to a charcoal disc, and allow it to smolder and release its fragrance.

*Romance and Attraction Incense*

**Herbs used:** Damiana, rose petals, cinnamon, and vanilla.

**Other ingredients:** Frankincense resin, charcoal.

**Purpose of the remedy:** This incense is designed to enhance romantic and sexual energy, and attract love.

**Instructions:**

1. Grind the herbs and frankincense resin into a fine powder using a mortar and pestle.
2. Add a small amount of the mixture to a charcoal disc, and allow it to smolder and release its fragrance.

*Meditation Incense*

**Herbs used:** Sandalwood, lavender, and frankincense.

**Other ingredients:** Charcoal.

**Purpose of the remedy:** This incense is designed to promote relaxation and enhance the meditative state.

**Instructions:**

1. Grind the herbs and frankincense resin into a fine powder using a mortar and pestle.
2. Add a small amount of the mixture to a charcoal disc, and allow it to smolder and release its fragrance.

### Inner Peace Incense

**Herbs used:** Lavender, chamomile, and rose petals.

**Other ingredients:** Frankincense resin, charcoal.

**Purpose of the remedy:** This incense is designed to promote inner peace and emotional balance.

**Instructions:**

1. Grind the herbs and frankincense resin into a fine powder using a mortar and pestle.
2. Add a small amount of the mixture to a charcoal disc, and allow it to smolder and release its fragrance.

*Divination Incense*

**Herbs used:** Mugwort, frankincense, and sandalwood.

**Other ingredients:** Charcoal.

**Purpose of the remedy:** This incense is designed to enhance psychic abilities and facilitate divination.

**Instructions:**

1. Grind the herbs and frankincense resin into a fine powder using a mortar and pestle.
2. Add a small amount of the mixture to a charcoal disc, and allow it to smolder and release its fragrance.

*Full Moon Incense*

**Herbs used:** Lavender, rose petals, and jasmine.

**Other ingredients:** Frankincense resin, charcoal.

**Purpose of the remedy:** This incense is designed to enhance the energy of the full moon and promote intuition and spiritual growth.

**Instructions:**

1. Grind the herbs and frankincense resin into a fine powder using a mortar and pestle.
2. Add a small amount of the mixture to a charcoal disc, and allow it to smolder and release its fragrance.

Overall, incense can be a powerful tool for enhancing and directing energy in rituals and spellwork. When you have prepared your own incense filled with your intentions you will feel a powerful difference in the quality of your practice.

Here are three of the most crucial things to refer back to when reviewing this chapter before making your own remedies:

1. You have explored a range of recipes for remedies and cures that are designed specifically for green witches who have grown their own herbs. These recipes provide a unique and powerful way to harness the healing properties of plants and incorporate them into your daily life.
2. By growing your own herbs, you have access to a diverse range of ingredients that can be used to treat a variety of ailments, from stress and

anxiety to headaches and digestive issues. You can also create customized blends that are tailored to your specific needs and preferences.

3. Whether you are making herbal tinctures, infused oils, teas, or candles, the process of preparing these remedies can be both meditative and empowering. By working with the plants in this way, you deepen your connection to nature and develop a greater appreciation for the healing power of the Earth.

In order to continue to grow and harvest the herbs that are used in these remedies, it is essential to care for and maintain your garden. The next chapter will focus on the best practices for maintaining a healthy and vibrant herb garden, including tips for soil preparation, watering and fertilization, pest control, and harvesting techniques. By taking care of your garden, you can ensure a steady supply of fresh and potent herbs for all of your herbal remedies and cures.

# CHAPTER 10
# CARING FOR YOUR MAGICKAL GARDEN

As Edwin Curran so eloquently said, "Flowers are the music of the ground. From Earth's lips spoken without sound" (Catherine, 2020). Starting a garden is a beautiful way to connect with the Earth and the spirits that dwell within it. As a Green Witch, you understand that gardening is an ongoing journey that requires commitment and responsibility. Once you start a garden, you are entering into a partnership with the nature spirits, and it is your responsibility to care for and maintain this sacred space. In this chapter, you will learn valuable tips and techniques for maintaining a healthy and thriving garden, ensuring that your plants continue to flourish and provide you with the healing remedies and cures that you need.

## WATERING YOUR PLANTS

Watering your plants may seem like a simple task, but it's actually more complicated than you may think. You want to ensure that your plants receive the proper amount of water to thrive and provide you with the healing properties you need. However, many people make common mistakes when it comes to watering their plants. In this chapter, we will discuss some of the most common watering mistakes people make and how to avoid them.

### *Watering at the Wrong Time of Day*

Watering at the wrong time of day is a common mistake that can have a significant impact on your plants. Watering during the hottest part of the day can cause the water to evaporate quickly and not reach the roots, leading to dehydration. Similarly, watering in the evening can cause excess moisture to accumulate, which can lead to fungal growth and other plant diseases. The best time to water your plants is in the early morning when the temperature is cooler, and the sun is not yet at its strongest.

### Watering the Tops of Plants

Another common mistake people make when watering their plants is watering the tops of the plants instead of the roots. Watering the tops of the plants may give the impression that you are providing enough water, but in reality, the water may not be reaching the roots, which is where the plants need it most. It's important to water at the base of the plant, allowing the water to seep into the soil and reach the roots.

### Over and Under Watering

Underwatering and overwatering are also common watering mistakes. Underwatering can cause the soil to become too dry, making it difficult for the plant to absorb nutrients and leading to dehydration. Overwatering, on the other hand, can cause the roots to become waterlogged, leading to root rot and other plant diseases. It's important to find a balance and water your plants only when they need it.

### Not Using Mulch (Outdoors)

When gardening outdoors, it's important to use mulch to help retain moisture in the soil. Mulch acts as a barrier, preventing water from evaporating too quickly and keeping the soil moist. Not using mulch can lead to your plants becoming dehydrated, especially during hot weather.

### Outdoors vs Indoors

It's also essential to differentiate between watering indoor and outdoor plants. Indoor plants typically require less water than outdoor plants, as they are not exposed to the elements. It's important to pay attention to the weather when gardening outdoors, as plants may require more water during hot, dry periods.

### Regular Watering

Watering your herbs regularly is essential to maintain their health and vitality. Be on the lookout for signs of wilting or drooping, as these are indications that your plants are thirsty. Pay attention to the moisture level of the soil, ensuring it's moist but not waterlogged. When watering, be sure to target the area around the herb and avoid getting water on the foliage, which can cause disease and rot. By taking note of changes in leaf color or texture, you can also detect if your plants are receiving the correct amount of water. Spend a few minutes each day with your herbs, observing how they respond to watering, sunlight, and other environmental factors.

### Build a Routine

It's important to establish a routine for watering your herbs that strikes a balance between over and underwatering. You want to avoid watering too frequently or too little, which can lead to root rot or drought stress. To develop a routine that works for you, start by observing your plants and noting how quickly they dry out. Watering during the early morning hours when it's cooler can help minimize water loss due to evaporation and prevent fungus growth. Watering at night can be harmful to your plants as it increases the chances of disease development and pests.

### Notice the Weather

Lastly, remember to adjust your watering routine according to weather changes, such as hot and dry periods, or prolonged rainy spells. By paying close attention to the moisture levels of your herbs and adjusting your watering routine as necessary, you'll be rewarded with healthy, thriving plants.

In conclusion, watering your plants is an important aspect of maintaining a healthy and thriving garden. By

210 • DELPHINA D'ANDRES

avoiding common watering mistakes, you can ensure that your plants receive the proper amount of water they need to flourish.

## WEEDING AND PRUNING

Keeping up with weeding and pruning is essential for maintaining the overall health and appearance of your herb garden. Weeds can quickly overrun your garden and steal nutrients from your herbs, so regular weeding is important to keep your herbs healthy and happy. Additionally, pruning your herbs helps to promote growth and ensures that your herbs are growing in a healthy and productive way. Pruning also helps to prevent your herbs from going to seed, which can limit their productivity and flavor. By taking the time to weed and prune your herbs, you'll not only keep your garden looking beautiful but also ensure that your herbs are thriving and producing to their fullest potential.

To keep your garden in good shape, it is important to check regularly for weeds and pull them out manually to prevent them from taking over. Planting your herbs closely together can also help minimize the chances of weeds growing. Pruning is another crucial aspect of herb garden maintenance. Starting early and pruning frequently can help prolong the life and output of your plants. Keep in mind that leafy herbs require more frequent pruning than woody herbs, which only need to be pruned once a year. When pruning, it is best to work from the top and remove larger leaves to allow for new growth. By following these tips, you can ensure that your herb garden remains healthy and visually pleasing.

## COMPOSTING

Composting is a crucial aspect of maintaining a healthy herb garden. Not only does it provide the necessary nutrients for your plants to grow, but it also helps retain moisture in the soil. When you compost, you create humus, which helps to enrich the soil and keep it healthy. Additionally, composting helps to keep pests and diseases in check, reducing the need for harmful chemical treatments.

To get started with composting, you should first decide on the type of compost that will best suit your garden's needs. For herb gardens, a compost with a balanced nitrogen-to-carbon ratio is ideal. This will ensure that the compost provides enough nutrients for your plants without becoming too acidic or alkaline. You can create your compost from a variety of materials, including fruit and vegetable scraps, grass clippings, and dried leaves.

Remember to turn your compost pile regularly to ensure that it is breaking down properly. This will help to create a healthy, nutrient-rich compost that will benefit your herb garden. By composting, you are not only improving the health of your garden, but also doing your part to reduce waste and contribute to a more sustainable environment.

### Helpful Tips

If you want to create good compost for your herb garden, there are a few tips to keep in mind. First, ensure you use a good balance of materials, including greens, browns, and nitrogen-rich materials. You can try hot composting, which can speed up the process of creating compost. Secondly, it is essential to cut up the ingredients into smaller pieces to speed up the decomposition process. Also, make sure you balance moisture levels by keeping the compost moist but not wet.

Hot composting is a process of breaking down organic materials into nutrient-rich compost by creating optimal conditions for microbes to thrive and break down the materials quickly. In hot composting, a mix of green and brown organic materials such as food waste, leaves, and grass clippings are layered together in a compost bin or pile, and then moistened and turned regularly to maintain aerobic conditions. As the materials decompose, the temperature inside the compost pile can reach up to 160°F (71°C), which helps to kill pathogens and weed seeds and speed up the breakdown process. Hot composting typically takes 1–3 months to produce finished compost that can be used to enrich soil and fertilize plants.

One useful tip for using your compost is to mix it with potting soil to boost the nutrient content. Another way to use your compost is as top-dressing around the base of your herb plants. This will help keep the soil moist, prevent erosion, and provide a slow release of nutrients to your plants. By following these composting tips, you can help ensure that your herb garden thrives and is a source of fresh, healthy herbs all season long.

## ATTRACTING THE RIGHT INSECTS

If you're looking to cultivate a healthy and thriving garden, it's important to understand the benefits of attracting beneficial insects. These insects, which include pollinators, predators, and parasitizers, can act as natural pest control by preying on other insects that might be harmful to your plants. Pollinators such as bees, butterflies, and moths help to fertilize plants, leading to more blooms and fruit production. Predators like ladybugs and praying mantises feed on plant-eating insects, while parasitizers like wasps lay their eggs on the larvae of these pests, killing them before they can cause any damage.

To attract beneficial insects to your garden, it's important to provide them with the right environment. This might include planting flowers that provide nectar and pollen for pollinators or adding a water source like a bird bath or fountain for insects to drink from. You can also use companion planting to attract specific types of beneficial insects, such as planting marigolds to attract ladybugs. Avoid using pesticides or other chemicals that could harm beneficial insects, and instead focus on creating a healthy and diverse ecosystem that will naturally attract these helpful creatures.

### Yarrow

Yarrow, with its fragrant flowers, attracts hoverflies and parasitic wasps that prey on aphids and other garden pests. Yarrow is easy to grow and thrives in well-drained soils, making it an excellent addition to any garden.

### Borage

Borage can be useful in attracting beneficial insects. Its beautiful blue flowers are popular with bees, and it is also known to attract parasitic wasps that prey on tomato hornworms and cabbage worms.

### Fennel

Fennel is also fantastic at attracting beneficial insects. It is known to attract ladybugs, lacewings, and hoverflies, all of which prey on aphids and other garden pests.

### Comfrey

Comfrey attracts predatory insects such as hoverflies and ladybugs. It is also known to improve soil quality, which can be beneficial for your plants.

### Anise Hyssop

Anise hyssop is a beautiful herb that can be grown in the garden to attract pollinators such as bees and butterflies. It is also known to attract beneficial insects such as hoverflies, which prey on aphids and other garden pests.

### Get to Know Your Insects

As you begin to cultivate your herb garden, take some time to observe the insects that are already present. Some may be beneficial, while others may be pests. By familiarizing yourself with the insects that are already in your garden, you can begin to make informed decisions about how to attract the right insects. Additionally, it's important to study which insects benefit which plants. Different plants attract different insects, and some insects are better suited for certain plants than others. By learning about these relationships, you can strategically plant herbs that will attract the beneficial insects that will help your garden thrive.

## WARDING OFF PESTS AND DISEASE

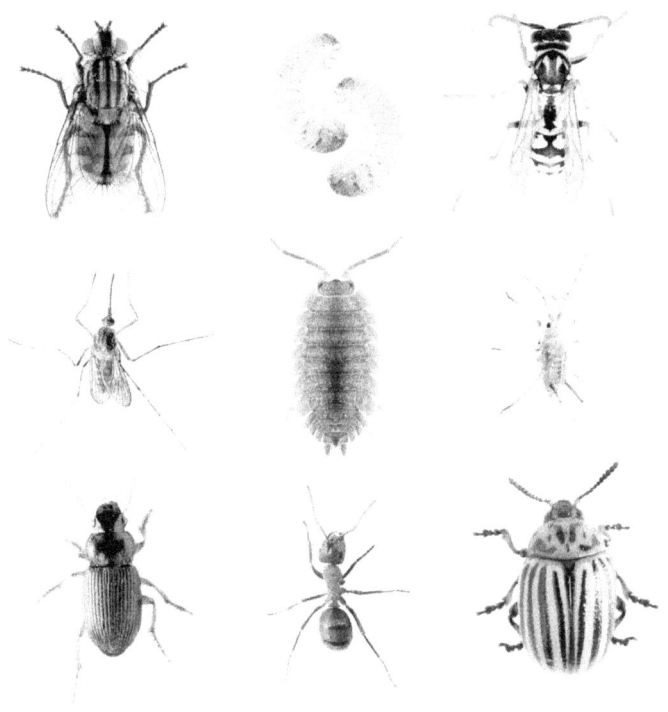

If you want to keep pests and diseases away from your herb garden, here are some tips that might come in handy. Firstly, try choosing plants that are known to repel pests. You can also use mulch to reduce watering needs, which can help prevent the spread of disease. If you bring in any new plants, it's a good idea to quarantine them to make sure they're not carrying any pests or diseases. Don't forget to clean up any debris or fallen leaves in your garden too! Pruning and not over-crowding your herb plants can also help to prevent problems. If you need to deter pests, try using natural concoctions like soap spray, neem oil, or essential oils. These can be very effective and are less harmful to the environment than synthetic pesticides.

Consider casting a circle with coffee grounds to create a barrier against negative energy. Decorate your garden with statues that represent protection or other symbols that are meaningful to you. You can also create penta-grams using sticks or other natural materials to ward off harmful energies. Hanging wind chimes is another way to create a protective barrier, as the sound they make is believed to deter negative spirits. Painting sigils on rocks and placing them around your garden is another way to bring protective energy to your space. You might also consider inviting fairies and other posi-tive spirits into your garden to help protect it. These magickal practices can help you protect your plants from pests and disease while also adding a unique and meaningful touch to your garden.

Here are three key points to focus on when caring for your magickal witchy garden:

1. Proper care and maintenance of a magickal garden involves regular weeding and pruning to keep the plants visually pleasing, stop them from going to seed, and prevent weeds from stealing nutrients.

2. Composting is an important aspect of caring for a magickal garden, as it provides the necessary nutrients for plant growth, helps retain moisture, and keeps pests and disease in check.

3. Attracting beneficial insects to the garden, using plants that repel pests, quarantining new plants, and using natural concoctions such as soap spray, neem oil, and essential oils are all effective ways to ward off pests and disease in a magickal garden.

You've come a long way in learning how to create and care for your own magickal garden. The next section, the conclusion, will tie together all the content you've covered so far and leave you with some final thoughts and inspiration to keep your garden thriving. Keep reading to complete your journey toward creating your own enchanting and vibrant garden.

# Help Another Witch!

Just as a thriving garden spreads its seeds, a good witch shares her knowledge... and now you've amped up yours, you're in a perfect position to help someone else.

Simply by sharing your honest opinion of this book, you'll show other green witches where they can find everything they need to plant and maintain a thriving magickal garden.

## TAKE A MOMENT TO SHARE YOUR THOUGHTS!

Thank you so much for your support. May your garden be abundant and magickal.

**Scan the QR code for a quick review!**

# CONCLUSION

Congratulations on completing this book on creating a magickal witch's garden! Throughout the various chapters, we've covered everything from the basics of herb gardening to the intricacies of making incense and teas.

By following the tips and techniques outlined in this book, you'll be able to create a beautiful, thriving garden that serves both your physical and spiritual needs.

To motivate you further, here's a success story: Jane, a busy accountant, thought she was too busy to start a garden. But after reading this book, she decided to give it a try. Starting with just a few herbs on her windowsill, she gradually expanded to a full garden in her backyard. It seems that once she got started, she found it so enlightening and enjoyable that she couldn't stop! She now enjoys the fruits of her labor, harvesting fresh herbs to add to her meals and incorporating them into her spellwork.

Remember, it's never too late to start a garden. With a little bit of patience and care, you can create a sacred space that nourishes your body and soul.

So, it's time to begin deciding where you want to create your sacred space and spreading your new-found knowledge to friends and acquaintances by sharing this book and leaving a review.

I wish you good luck on your journey towards creating your magickal witch's garden. May it bring you joy, peace, and abundance!

# REFERENCES

Adelmann, M. (2013, May 6). *How to make herb-infused oils.* Herbal Academy. https://theherbalacademy.com/herb-infused-oils/

*Beginners guide to companion planting.* (n.d.). Heeman's. https://www. heeman.ca/garden-guides/companion-planting/

Beyer, C. (2018, April 13). *Definition of left and right hand paths in occultism.* Learn Religions. https://www.learnreligions.com/left-hand-and-right-hand-paths-95827

Campus, J. (2019, November 25). *Create a custom garden full of magical plants in 8 easy steps.* Garden and Happy. https://gardenandhappy. com/magical-plants/

Casley, N. (2021, March 30). *5 common watering mistakes you are probably making.* Bokashi Experts. https://bokashiliving.com/5-common-watering-mistakes-you-are-probably-making/

Catherine. (2020, December 21). *60 inspirational gardening quotes and garden sayings.* Growing Family. https://growingfamily.co.uk/garden-tips/60-inspirational-gardening-quotes-garden-sayings/

*Create a stunning herb container garden.* (n.d.). HGTV. https://www.hgtv. com/outdoors/landscaping-and-hardscaping/create-a-stunning-herb-container-garden

Dekker, S. (2022, May 4). *Tips for companion planting in your herb garden.* Gardener's Path. https://gardenerspath.com/plants/herbs/compan ion-planting/

Duford, M. J. (2022, March 30). *10 witch garden tips to cultivate and nurture sacred space.* Home for the Harvest. https://www.home fortheharvest.com/create-a-witch-garden/ #4_Grow_witchy_plants

Ehrenreich, B. (2022, October 19). *Herbalists and witches: A brief history.* Prairie Star Botanicals. https://prairiestarbotanicals.com/blogs/news/herbalist-and-witches-a-brief-history

*8 balcony herb garden ideas you would like to try.* (2015, August 21).

Balcony Garden Web. https://balconygardenweb.com/8-balcony-herb-garden-ideas-you-would-like-to-try/

*8 simple, homemade herbal tea recipes.* (2020, March 17). Simple Loose Leaf Tea Company. https://simplelooseleaf.com/blog/herbal-tea/herbal-tea-recipes/

farmtheworld. (2019, April 10). *10 essential gardening tools (Plus a few extras that we love).* Farm the World. https://farmtheworld.org/2019/04/10/essential-gardening-tools/

Fletcher, J. (2019, January 10). *Herbal tinctures: 6 types and recipes.* Medical News Today. https://www.medicalnewstoday.com/articles/324149#recipe

Gardiner, B. (n.d.). *Stress relief tea - Hot infusion.* Outdoor Apothecary. https://www.outdoorapothecary.com/wprm_print/4788

Garis, M. G., & Norris, R. (2023, January 9). *I'm a green witch, and I swear by these 7 herbs for healing and self care.* Well+Good. https://www.wellandgood.com/herbs-for-emotional-healing/

Goddess Garden. (2019, May 31). *How to create an altar or sacred space.* The Goddess Garden. https://thegoddessgarden.com/how-to-create-an-altar-or-sacred-space/

*Growing a witch's garden - Seeds from alchemy works.* (n.d.). Alchemy-Works. https://www.alchemy-works.com/witchs_garden.html

*Guide to homemade medicine: Healing tinctures and tonics.* (2023, January 6). Academy of Culinary Nutrition. https://www.culinarynutrition.com/how-to-make-tinctures-and-tonics/

*A guide to watering herbs—Best practices for a healthy herb garden.* (2022, August 28). Swan Hose. https://swanhose.com/blogs/watering-herbs/a-guide-to-watering-herbs-best-practices-for-a-healthy-herb-garden

Haare, K. D. (2017, December 8). *DIY hand poured herbal candles.* Herbal Academy. https://theherbalacademy.com/hand-poured-herbal-candles/

Harris, K. (2022, November 7). *32 inspirational gardening quotes.* Treehugger. https://www.treehugger.com/inspirational-gardening-quotes-4868813

Hepler, J. (2020, June). *Natural pest control: Attracting beneficial insects.*

Piedmont Master Gardeners. https://piedmontmastergardeners. org/article/natural-pest-control-attracting-beneficial-insects/

Herb Exchange. (2021, August 10). *7 common herb gardening mistakes & how to avoid them*. The Herb Exchange. https://theherbexchange. com/7-common-herb-gardening-mistakes/

*Herbs and tools for energetic protection*. (2022, April 8). Anima Mundi Herbals. https://animamundiherbals.com/blogs/blog/herbs-and-tools-for-energetic-protection

Herman, M, and Driessen, S. (n.d.). *Preserving herbs by freezing or drying*. University of Minnesota. https://extension.umn.edu/preserving-and-preparing/preserving-herbs-freezing-or-drying

*The history of green witchcraft*. (2020, July 7). Letters to Lilith. https:// www.letterstolilith.com/blog/the-history-of-green-witchcraft

*How to attract fairies*. (2020, December 1). Grounded in the Earth. https://groundedintheEarth.com/how-to-attract-faeries-to-your-garden

*How to grow herbs: A step-by-step guide - Back to the roots*. (2020, December 2). Back to the Roots. https://blog.backtotheroots.com/ 2020/12/02/how-to-grow-herbs/

*How to prune your herb garden using the right pruning tool*. (2022, August 18). ECOgardener. https://ecogardener.com/blogs/news/how-to-prune-your-herb-garden

Huffman, T. (n.d.). *How to plant an herb container garden for patio or kitchen*. Greenhouse Studio. https://www.greenhousestudio.co/ home-garden/how-plant-herb-container-garden

Jabbour, N. (2021, June 18). *How to harvest herbs: How and when to harvest homegrown herbs*. Savvy Gardening. https://savvygardening. com/how-to-harvest-herbs/

Jay, S. (2023, January 9). *Herbs for protection: 16 plants to strengthen your boundaries*. Revoloon. https://revoloon.com/shanijay/herbs-for-protection

Jodi. (n.d.). *Companion planting chart for herbs*. Farm Homestead. https:// farmhomestead.com/gardening-methods/companion-planting-chart-herbs/

Knight, M. (2019, July 22). *How to create a witch's garden - Beginner gardening tips for witches.* Mookychick. https://www.mookychick.co. uk/health/witchcraft-spirituality/how-to-create-a-witchs-garden-beginner-gardening-tips-for-witches.php

Kristen. (2023, February 18). *15 best herbs for protection.* Schisandra & Bergamot. https://schisandraandbergamot.com/herbs-for-protection/

Kuczykowski, T. (2022, March 24). *10-minute easy DIY indoor herb planter.* Unsophisticook. https://unsophisticook.com/easy-indoor-herb-garden/

Lynn. (2011, February 9). *Lunar herb gardening.* Urban Herbology. https://urban-herbology.org/2011/02/09/lunar-herb-gardening/

Masley, S., and Crain, A. (2021, December 15). *How to prepare soil for planting herbs: 12 steps (With pictures).* WikiHow. https://www.wiki how.life/Prepare-Soil-for-Planting-Herbs

McGruther, J. (2019, July 10). *How to make a stinging nettle infusion for adrenal support and allergy relief.* Nourished Kitchen. https://nour ishedkitchen.com/stinging-nettle-infusion/

McGruther, J. (2022a, March 21). *Four thieves vinegar.* Nourished Kitchen. https://nourishedkitchen.com/four-thieves-vinegar-recipe/

McGruther, J. (2022b, October 20). *Pregnancy tea recipe.* Nourished Kitchen. https://nourishedkitchen.com/pregnancy-tea-recipe/

McLaughlin, C. (2010, January 5). *Basic gardening tools 101.* FineGardening. https://www.finegardening.com/article/basic-gardening-tools-101

McLeod, D. (2016, August 9). *The best indoor herb garden ideas you can grow at home.* Backyard Boss. https://www.backyardboss.net/indoor-herb-garden-ideas/

Monaghan, P. (2012, May 28). *Inviting fairies into your garden.* Llewellyn Worldwide. https://www.llewellyn.com/journal/article/2291

moodymoons. (2020, January 6). *7 easy incense recipes for any magic spell.* Moody Moons. https://www.moodymoons.com/2020/01/06/7-easy-incense-recipes-for-any-magic-spell/

*The moon's phases.* (2014, February 13). Green Witch. https://www.greenwitch.ca/moon-phases/

Muckle, S. (2016, June 1). *Plant folklore: Myths, magic, and superstition.* Gardener's Path. https://gardenerspath.com/plants/plant-folklore/

Nate. (2021, July 16). *Potting mix for herbs and vegetables.* Get Urban Leaf. https://www.geturbanleaf.com/blogs/supplies/potting-mix-for-herbs-and-vegetables

*Nature, spirits, devas, elementals.* (n.d.). Crystalinks. https://www.crystalinks.com/nature_spirits.html

Netzer, J. (2023, April 24). *What is a green witch? The beginner's guide to embracing earthly magick.* Cratejoy Subscription Box Marketplace. https://www.cratejoy.com/box-insider/green-witch-primer/

Olcese, A. (2020, August 24). *6 herbs to grow for emotional health.* Mother Earth Living. https://www.motherEarthliving.com/gardening/herb-gardening/emotional-health-herbs-zm0z17jazolc/

Olivia. (2020, September 4). *How we harvest our herbs based on seasons + the moon's cycle.* Organic Olivia. https://blog.organicolivia.com/how-we-harvest-our-herbs-based-on-seasons-the-moons-cycle/

Pivarnik, M. (2019, May 10). *Spiritual heart medicine: How to use herbs for emotional self-care.* Herbal Academy. https://theherbalacademy.com/emotional-self-care-herbs/

*Planting by the moon and stars: Great idea or hogwash?* (2021, January 15). The Grow Network. https://thegrownetwork.com/planting-by-the-moon/

*Planting herbs & propagating by cuttings.* (n.d.). Planet Natural. https://www.planetnatural.com/herb-gardening-guru/planting/

Plantwalker, M. (2023, April 25). *Essential gardening tools for the home gardener.* Chestnut School of Herbal Medicine. https://chestnutherbs.com/essential-gardening-tools-for-the-home-gardener/

Pollux, A. (2019, December 11). *Create a magical witch's garden with our 17 top pointers.* WiccaNow. https://wiccanow.com/create-a-witchs-garden-with-our-17-top-pointers/

*Powerful herbs for emotional and spiritual healing.* (2021, December 28). Original Botanica. https://originalbotanica.com/blog/best-herbs-emotional-healing

Reaney, H. (2022, June 10). *Herb garden ideas – 18 ways to grow an aromatic crop, indoors and outdoors.* Homes and Gardens. https://www.homesandgardens.com/ideas/herb-garden-ideas

Rhoads, H. (2021, July 6). *Growing herbs at home: Making an herb garden in your yard.* Gardening Know How. https://www.gardeningknowhow.com/edible/herbs/hgen/plant-herb-garden.htm

Rosalee. (n.d.). *Lemon balm tea.* Herbal Remedies Advice. https://www.herbalremediesadvice.org/lemon-balm-tea.html

Rose, S. (2021, January 27). *Designing the vegetable garden: How to make a garden map.* Garden Therapy. https://gardentherapy.ca/garden-map/

Russell, D. (2020, July 30). *Green witchcraft for mental, emotional, & spiritual healing.* Davy and Tracy. https://davyandtracy.com/spirituality/green-witchcraft/

Sedhoff, D. W. (2020, April 26). *5 ways to enhance your spirituality and connect with nature.* Mindfood. https://www.mindfood.com/article/5-ways-to-enhance-your-spirituality-and-connect-with-nature/

Sell, J. (2016, October 24). *Witchery in the garden.* Lady Bird Johnson Wildflower Center. https://www.wildflower.org/magazine/native-plants/witchery-in-the-garden

Smith, E. W. (2022, July 11). *Witch quotes to help you get in touch with your magickal side.* Cosmopolitan. https://www.cosmopolitan.com/lifestyle/a35302526/best-witch-quotes/

*Soil for herbs - All components explained - How I make my own potting mix.* (n.d.). Amazing Herb Garden. https://www.amazingherbgarden.com/best-soil-for-herbs-how-to-make-your-own-potting-mix/#goodpottingsoil

Sproule, R. (2019, May 9). *Moon phase gardening.* Salisbury Greenhouse. https://salisburygreenhouse.com/moon-phase-gardening/

Stallsmith, A. (2022, June 23). *7 important things to know about growing herbs outdoors.* Bob Vila. https://www.bobvila.com/articles/growing-herbs-outdoors/

*The story.* (n.d.). The Witches Garden. https://thewitchesgarden.com/?page_id=673

Svedi, R. (2021, June 14). *General care for your herb garden.* Gardening

Know How. https://www.gardeningknowhow.com/edible/herbs/hgen/general-care-for-your-herb-garden.htm

Svedi, R. (2021, June 25). *StackPath*. Gardening Know How. https://www.gardeningknowhow.com/edible/herbs/hgen/choosing-a-site-for-your-herb-garden.htm

Thompson, H. (2014, October 31). *How witches' brews helped bring modern drugs to market*. Smithsonian Magazine. https://www.smithsonianmag.com/science-nature/how-witches-brews-helped-bring-modern-drugs-market-180953202/

*Top 10 magickal herbs.* (n.d.). Tamed Wild. https://us14.campaign-archive.com/?u=f240a7ed96281fbf13d16d758&id=552777243e

Trees.com Staff. (2022, December 22). *25 pretty herb garden ideas*. Trees. https://www.trees.com/gardening-and-landscaping/herb-garden-ideas

*20 simple herbal recipes for teas, tinctures, shrubs and more.* (n.d.). Nourished Kitchen. https://nourishedkitchen.com/herbalism/

*The ultimate guide to composting for a herb garden.* (2023, March 15). CompostHQ. https://composthq.com/composting/how-to-create-compost-for-a-herb-garden/

Undlin, S. (n.d.). *15 healing herbs you can grow at home*. Earth. https://www.Earth.com/Earthpedia-articles/15-healing-herbs-you-can-grow-at-home

Vinje, E. (2019, June 29). *Gardening 101: Planning and design guide*. Planet Natural. https://www.planetnatural.com/garden-planning/

Virginia. (2022a, January 8). *10 easy kitchen herb garden ideas to grow culinary herbs*. The Culinary Herb Garden. https://howtoculinaryherbgarden.com/herb-garden-ideas/

Virginia. (2022b, March 15). *Herb gardening containers: Selecting the right herb pots and planters*. The Culinary Herb Garden. https://howtoculinaryherbgarden.com/outdoor-herb-pots/

Wachtel-Galor, S., & Benzie, I. F. F. (2011). *Herbal medicine*. Nih.gov; CRC Press/Taylor & Francis. https://www.ncbi.nlm.nih.gov/books/NBK92773/

Waddington, E. (2021, July 21). *12 easy & inexpensive space-saving herb garden ideas.* Rural Sprout. https://www.ruralsprout.com/space-saving-herb-gardens/

Ward, K. (2022, August 26). *Yeah, there's not just \*one\* type of witch —There are tons of them.* Cosmopolitan. https://www.cosmopolitan.com/lifestyle/a37681530/types-of-witches/

Washington, K. (2019, April 13). *Kitchen witch: Growing herbs.* Edible Communities. https://www.ediblecommunities.com/home-cooking/kitchen-witch/growing-herbs/

*What is a green witch?* (n.d.). Naturally Modern. https://naturallymodernlife.com/what-is-a-green-witch/

*A wiccan guide to moon magic.* (n.d.). Wicca Living. https://wiccaliving.com/wiccan-full-moon-ritual/

Wigington, P. (2018, May 15). *How to harvest, dry, and store your magical herbs.* Learn Religions. https://www.learnreligions.com/harvesting-drying-and-storing-magical-herbs-2562025

Windheart, N. (2021, September 29). *Fairy tree: Making space for the nature spirits.* Nancy Windheart. https://nancywindheart.com/fairy-tree-making-space-for-the-nature-spirits/

*Witchcraft quotes.* (n.d.). Notable Quotes. https://www.notable-quotes.com/w/witchcraft_quotes.html

Wolfe, S. E. (2022a, September 14). *Protection magick for your witch's garden.* Green Witch Living. https://blog.greenwitchliving.com/protection-magick-witchs-garden/

Wolfe, S. E. (2022b, September 29). *Witchy DIYs: Make your own incense blends.* Green Witch Living. https://blog.greenwitchliving.com/make-your-own-incense-blends/

WTHN Team. (2020, June 11). *Herbs for energy: Ditch the caffeine with these 7 herbs.* WTHN. https://wthn.com/blogs/wthnside-out/herbs-for-energy

## IMAGE REFERENCES

*Angelica.* (n.d.). Vista Print. https://99designs.com/projects/1564761/files/100

Artmim. (n.d.). *Woman with tea cup on background of blurred green leaves.* Shutterstock. https://www.shutterstock.com/image-photo/woman-tea-cup-on-background-blurred-128069681

*Bay leaves.* (n.d.). Vista Print. https://99designs.com/projects/1564761/files/85

Bogdanski, S. (n.d.). *Olibanum.* Shutterstock. https://www.shutterstock.com/image-photo/olibanum-20512625

Brebca. (n.d.). *Outdoor flower pots for small garden, patio or terrace.* Deposit Photos. https://depositphotos.com/70142057/stock-photo-flower-pots.html

*Chamomile.* (n.d.). Vista Print. https://99designs.com/projects/1564761/files/93

*Chives.* (n.d.). Vista Print. https://99designs.com/projects/1564761/files/120

*Comfrey.* (n.d.). Vista Print. https://99designs.com/projects/1564761/files/103

Crawford, C. (2021, June 21). *Summer spell candles, hand-dipped by The Self-Care Emporium.* Unsplash. https://unsplash.com/photos/qbDF0LDGq4w

Croisby. (n.d.). *Antique style hand drawn line art and dot work moon phases circle. Boho chic poster, tattoo, altar veil or tapestry design vector illustration.* Shutterstock. https://www.shutterstock.com/image-vector/antique-style-hand-drawn-line-art-1395036494

Elenathewise. (n.d.). *Various dried medicinal herbs and herbal teas in several glass jars on gray wood background, close up.* Deposit Photos. https://depositphotos.com/170609136/stock-photo-fried-herbs-in-jars.html

*Eleuthero.* (n.d.). Vista Print. https://99designs.com/projects/1564761/files/113

*Feverfew.* (n.d.). Vista Print. https://99designs.com/projects/1564761/files/118

*Geranium.* (n.d.). Vista Print. https://99designs.com/projects/1564761/files/104

GoodStudio. (n.d.). *Urban gardening collection. People living in city cultivating plants, growing crops or vegetables in pots at home or on balcony isolated on white background. Colorful hand drawn vector illustration.* Shutterstock. https://www.shutterstock.com/image-vector/urban-gardening-collection-people-living-city-1136033342

*Hibiscus.* (n.d.). Vista Print. https://99designs.com/projects/1564761/files/106

*Holy basil.* (n.d.). Vista Print. https://99designs.com/projects/1564761/files/117

*Hops.* (n.d.). Vista Print. https://99designs.com/projects/1564761/files/111

*Horsetail.* (n.d.). Vista Print. https://99designs.com/projects/1564761/files/98

*Hyssop.* (n.d.). Vista Print. https://99designs.com/projects/1564761/files/95

Ju_See. (n.d.). *Magic is in you - inspiration quote. minerals, candles and books on table, abstract dark background. Healing crystal ritual for relax, meditation. wiccan witchcraft, spiritual esoteric practice.* Shutterstock. https://www.shutterstock.com/image-photo/magic-you-inspiration-quote-minerals-candles-1462563353

Julia_Arda. (n.d.). *Eco friendly wooden house model in green grass, daisies chamomile flower, ladybug sitting on leaf, ecological sustainable lifestyle, life harmony. Buying or selling real estate, investment concept.* Deposit Photos. https://depositphotos.com/369727784/stock-photo-eco-friendly-wooden-house-model.html

*Lavender.* (n.d.). Vista Print. https://99designs.com/projects/1564761/files/107

*Lemon.* (n.d.). Vista Print. https://99designs.com/projects/1564761/files/108

*Lemon balm.* (n.d.). Vista Print. https://99designs.com/projects/1564761/files/102

*Lemon grass.* (n.d.). Vista Print. https://99designs.com/projects/ 1564761/files/122

Marjogaine. (n.d.). *3d computer graphics of a flying fairy with blond hair and butterfly wings.* Deposit Photos. https://depositphotos.com/ 40436229/stock-photo-sunshine-flyer-3d-cg.html

*Mandrake root.* (n.d.). Vista Print. https://99designs.com/projects/ 1564761/files/87

*Mugwort.* (n.d.). Vista Print. https://99designs.com/projects/1564761/ files/92

*Myrrh.* (n.d.). Vista Print. https://99designs.com/projects/1564761/ files/97

*Nettle.* (n.d.). Vista Print. https://99designs.com/projects/1564761/ files/99

Nunochka. (n.d.). *Harvesting herbs of oregano and tutsan into bundles and preparation for drying concept. Methods of preservation for herbs or flowers for future use.* Deposit Photos. https://depositphotos.com/ 404448066/stock-photo-harvesting-herbs-of-oregano-and.html

OlezzoSimona. (n.d.). *Body cream and plant on wooden table.* Deposit Photos. https://depositphotos.com/40063191/stock-photo-body-cream-and-wildflowers-on.html

*Oregano.* (n.d.). Vista Print. https://99designs.com/projects/1564761/ files/121

*Panax ginseng.* (n.d.). Vista Print. https://99designs.com/projects/ 1564761/files/90

PandaWild. (n.d.). *Moon 30 day phases.* Deposit Photos. https://deposit photos.com/127891246/stock-photo-moon-30-day-phases.html

*Parsley.* (n.d.). Vista Print. https://99designs.com/projects/1564761/ files/119

*Passionflower.* (n.d.). Vista Print. https://99designs.com/projects/ 1564761/files/112

*Peppermint.* (n.d.). Vista Print. https://99designs.com/projects/ 1564761/files/86

*Pseudostellaria.* (n.d.). Vista Print. https://99designs.com/projects/ 1564761/files/114

*Rhodiola root.* (n.d.). Vista Print. https://99designs.com/projects/

1564761/files/115

*Rosemary.* (n.d.). Vista Print. https://99designs.com/projects/1564761/ files/101

*Roses.* (n.d.). Vista Print. https://99designs.com/projects/1564761/ files/105

*Rue.* (n.d.). Vista Print. https://99designs.com/projects/1564761/ files/88

*Sage.* (n.d.). Vista Print. https://99designs.com/projects/1564761/ files/91

*Schisandra.* (n.d.). Vista Print. https://99designs.com/projects/ 1564761/files/116

*Skullcap.* (n.d.). Vista Print. https://99designs.com/projects/1564761/ files/110

Srihawog, P. (n.d.). *Gardening concept. A young woman mixes potting soil, prepares the soil for planting vegetables and herbs in the house, mixes potting soil, perlite, vermiculite, peat, worm, coconut flakes, rice husk.* Shutterstock. https://www.shutterstock.com/image-photo/garden ing-concept-young-woman-mixes-potting-2225273901

*St John's wort.* (n.d.). Vista Print. https://99designs.com/projects/ 1564761/files/96

*Thyme.* (n.d.). Vista Print. https://99designs.com/projects/1564761/ files/94

Toa55. (n.d.). *Garden design.* Shutterstock. https://www.shutterstock. com/image-photo/garden-design-148432271

*Valerian.* (n.d.). Vista Print. https://99designs.com/projects/1564761/ files/109

Vladvitek. (n.d.). *Garden pests. Collection of the insects on a white back-ground.* Deposit Photos. https://depositphotos.com/66001905/ stock-photo-collection-of-the-insects.html

Wilkes, S. (2019, September 7). *Misty woodland illuminated by sunlight on a summer's morning, Richmond Park, London.* Unsplash. https:// unsplash.com/photos/2ceyL8qAPXg

*Wormwood.* (n.d.). Vista Print. https://99designs.com/projects/ 1564761/files/89

Zoinerek. (n.d.). *Natural medicine concept. Vintage pharmacist preparing natural medicament. Brass mortar and bottles. Rustic table. Assorted dry herbs in bowls.* Deposit Photos. https://depositphotos.com/347194698/stock-photo-natural-medicine-concept-vintage-pharmacist.html